The Daring Destination

The Story of a God-given Dream Becoming a Reality

Kristie Chute

All Scripture quotations are taken from *The Holy Bible: New International Version®* NIV®. Copyright © 1973, 1978, 1984 by International Bible Society. Used by permission of Zondervan Publishing House. All rights reserved.

Copyright © 2017 Kristie Chute

ISBN: 978-193652111-1

All rights reserved under international copyright law. No part of this book may be reproduced or transmitted in any form or by any means, graphic, electronic, digital or mechanical, including photocopying, recording, taping, or by any information storage retrieval system, without the permission in writing from the author.

This book is dedicated to my parents—Tim and Tammie Chute. Thank you for being my heroes, biggest cheerleaders, and the two greatest influences in my life.

Contents

Authors Note 7
Chapter 1: Where It All Began 11
Chapter 2: Be Careful What You Pray For 19
Chapter 3: Once, Okay. Twice . . . No Way. 29
Chapter 4: Get Up & Go. 37
Chapter 5: Prep Time 49
Chapter 6: Not A Cake Walk 57
Chapter 7: Too Late To Turn Back Now 65
Chapter 8: Haters Gonna Hate 75
Chapter 9: Joy Comes in the Morning 87
Chapter 10: In His Hands 95
Chapter 11: Open Doors 103
Chapter 12: Bold Prayers 111
Chapter 13: A Divine Meeting 119
Chapter 14: You Gotta Know Who You Are 129
Chapter 15: Things Just Got Real 139
Chapter 16: The Cat is All The Way Out of The Bag 151
Chapter 17: What Faith Can Do 163
Chapter 18: Dreams Do Come True 173

Chapter 19: Under the Influence	193
Chapter 20: In His Strength	205
Chapter 21: Keep Dreamin'	215
The Next Step	225
Acknowledgments	227
About the Author	231
Connect with Kristie!	233

Authors Note

Dear Reader,

First off, thank you for picking up this book! It has always been one of my life long dreams to write a book, so thank you for making that possible by getting a copy. I sincerely hope you are inspired, motivated, and challenged by what you are about to read in the following pages.

Throughout my life so far, I have had many dreams. But, if I could sum up my purpose and ultimate dream in one statement, it would be this: To accomplish and live out my God given dreams and then encourage, equip, and inspire others to go out and live theirs.

My deepest prayer is for this book to do just that.

I pray you are deeply encouraged as you read my story and the journey God took me on to accomplish my God-given dream. I pray you begin to realize the dreams God has put in your heart, which seem so big, so scary, and so far away are maybe a lot closer than you think. I pray you recognize your dreams, which may seem impossible, are truly possible with God.

I pray that as you flip through and read these pages you can find yourself in my story—an ordinary person with an extraordinary call of God on your life. Yes, the call will be intimidating and overwhelming. Yes, you will feel lost and confused at times. Yes, you will have times of disbelief and despair. But, believe me, it will be so worth it. There is no better feeling than living out what God has put you on this earth to do. Trust me, the good times will out weigh the bad. You'll learn how to trust God like never before. You'll see yourself grow in your relationship with the Lord as you slowly begin to start following after His plan. You'll watch God work out situations and provide in ways that blow your mind.

I pray that this story will challenge you to say "yes!" to the big dreams that God has placed on your heart, and after reading it, I pray you will feel encouraged, equipped, and inspired to go out and live those dreams.

Enjoy! And thank you.
Kristie Chute

"When God gives you a dream, hold onto that dream, and God will hold onto you."

-Dr. Mark Rutland

Chapter 1

Where It All Began

I have always considered myself a dreamer. I have always loved hearing stories of people like Mother Teresa, Martin Luther King Jr., or Joseph in the Bible—all people who had enormous dreams and many obstacles to overcome. I have always been fascinated by people with big dreams who beat the odds, crossed the finish line, reached their mountain top, the destination they had strived to arrive at for such a long time. I have always dreamed about what God could do through my one life and prayed He would instill big dreams inside of me.

For as long as I can remember, I dreamed of being a missionary. I grew up going to a private, Christian school that had weekly chapel services. When I was in the first grade, a missionary to the Philippines was the speaker at one particular chapel service. She shared stories and pictures from her missionary journeys. As she was speaking, an excitement began to stir in my heart. At six years old, sitting in that chapel service, I remember hearing the voice of God speak to me for the first time. As this woman was speaking about her mission trips, God spoke to me and said, "Kristie, that's what I want you to do. I want you to go around the world and tell people about me." It was as simple as that, but hearing the voice of God for the first time that day helped establish a foundation for the direction of my life.

After hearing God speak to me, I was so excited! I ran up to my first grade teacher at the end of the service and told her God was calling me to be a missionary. Tears began to roll down her face, and she took me to the missionary for prayer. After school, I went home and told my parents God was calling me to be a missionary. They were supportive, but they probably figured it would not stick long considering I wanted to be a doctor, cashier, and librarian all the week before I had this revelation! But, I knew in my heart that something was different, and ever since that first grade chapel service, I grew up dreaming of becoming a missionary, and I have never looked back!

By the time I was 12, I was begging my parents to let me go on my first missions trip. I thought I was old enough to go to a third world nation by myself for a whole week. My parents seemed to have very different thoughts on the matter.

Year 13 rolled around, and another opportunity arose for me to go on a missions trip, but soon after my hopes were lifted, they began to fade as those plans fell through.

By the time I was 14, I was more ready than ever to head out to the missions field. I was sitting in a youth conference in the early spring of my eighth grade year. During the conference, a man got on stage and started talking about missions and how important it was to go into the world proclaiming the Gospel. While the man was speaking, I heard the voice of the Lord speak to me. I heard the still small voice of the Holy Spirit whisper to my heart saying, "Kristie, this is your year. You're going to go on a missions trip to Guatemala this summer." I thought to myself, Finally!

When I got home, I excitedly told my parents what God had said. After some thought and prayer, they told me I could sign up for the Guatemala trip. My mom still admits to me today that the only reason she said I could sign up was because she thought I would never raise the money to go! But, despite some of the doubt, the money came in, and before I knew it, I had all the funds I needed to go on the trip! There was only one problem. We were about a week out from the trip and my passport had not been delivered to me yet. There was no way I was getting into Guatemala or getting back into the United States without a passport…that is a pretty nonnegotiable issue!

If my passport did not arrive within a couple of days, I would miss out on the trip I had worked so hard to raise the money for. I remember thinking, there is no way I am going to let a passport stop me from going on this trip. That week, I constantly prayed that my passport would arrive on time. All my friends and family were praying. I would wake up in the middle of the night, get on my knees by my bedside, and pray for it to come in time.

There were only two days left before my team was supposed to leave for Guatemala, and my passport still was nowhere to be found. I remember feeling so confused. I thought, Maybe it was not God who said I was supposed to be on this trip? Maybe I just made that up because I wanted to go on a mission trip so desperately? I thought, Man, I was so sure God wanted me on this trip. Despite the doubts, I still prayed and believed God was going to provide a miracle.

Saturday came, and our team was scheduled to fly out on Sunday morning. On Saturday afternoon, my doorbell rang. I opened the door to find a FedEx deliveryman holding a small package in his hand with my passport inside. I jumped for joy and hugged the deliveryman! (He was probably confused as to what was going on). "Thank you! Thank you! Thank you!" I shouted, and then a dance party started around my house as soon as I closed the front door! It was the day before the trip and my God had come through!

I was about to go on my first missions trip—something I had dreamed about for years! God provided a miracle by allowing my passport to show up less than 24 hours before I was supposed to leave the country, and I knew this was even further confirmation that God wanted me to go on that trip! I was more expectant than ever that the week ahead would be a life-changing week. Looking back, I can say with full confidence my first missions trip was a game changer, and it set me on the course I would be on for the rest of my life.

Sitting here at 22 years old, I still remember exactly how I felt after the first night of ministry in Guatemala. Our team went to minster to a local church, and at the end of the service, our team had the chance to lay hands on people and pray for them. The people who needed prayer were told to come to the front and nearly 85 percent of the congregation came forward. At fourteen, I had never laid hands on someone to pray for them, but I had always wanted to. I remember thinking, Well, I don't know what I'm doing, but I am just going to simply pray like I know how to pray. I went to the front, and the first man I saw, I began to pray for. While I was praying for him, the presence of the Holy Spirit came, and it came on so overwhelmingly strong, this man fell to the floor. He was slain in the Holy Spirit. I was in complete awe! I began to understand that God could move through me, a little fourteen-year-old girl? It seemed crazy, but it was awesome! I kept moving through the crowd, laying hands on different people. The presence of God was all over the room. Hardly anyone who was prayed for was left standing. I could not believe what I was witnessing, but even more than that, I could not fathom that God would pick me, a young, inexperienced, newbie to work through.

After the church service was over and everyone left, I remember sitting on the steps of the stage trying to process what I had just witnessed. I had never felt the presence of God or seen God move so strongly before in my life. I sat on the stage steps, and I remember saying quietly to myself, "Wow, there is nothing else I want to do for the rest of my life. This is what life is all about, and if I give my life to doing this, to seeing lives be touched and transformed by the presence of God, I will be so happy. That's all I need. This is all I want to do for the rest of my life."

I cannot help but tear up as I write this because I still feel the exact same way today. Nothing brings me more joy than seeing people who are full of hopelessness and despair lay their burdens down at the feet of Jesus. Still, nothing makes me more excited than when God moves through me to touch someone else's life and bring them back to Him. Looking back, I now see that sitting on those steps, at fourteen years old, I had discovered my purpose, and once you taste purpose, it's hard, no it's nearly impossible, to turn back.

I will never forget my first missions trip to Guatemala. The rest of the week only got better, and I fell in love with the missions field. God used me and my team in ways that completely blew my mind. Personally, he worked through me to see miracles I never even imagined I would see in my lifetime, much less at 14. After the week trip, I knew without a doubt it was God I heard speak to me, telling me He was calling me to be a missionary, when I was six. I came off that week excited about everything God had done and eager to discover all the possibilities the future held.

As beautiful as all of this was, my story was only beginning.

Personal Journal Entry

June 24, 2007

Oh my gosh! Today was the best day ever! We went to a church service that had about 250 people, and we got to pray for them at the end! When the speaker asked for people to come forward if they needed prayer, almost the entire congregation came forward! The first man I prayed for was slain in the Holy Spirit… through me! A fourteen-year-old girl! I will definitely remember that moment for the rest of my life. It's crazy how God can use me to do something like that. I went down the line and continued to pray for people, and they kept getting slain in the Spirit! It was one of the best times of my life. When I prayed for each person, I would walk up to them, and God would reveal to me what was wrong with them and what they needed prayer for. For example, I walked up to one lady and started to pray for her. While I was praying, God told me that she needed a breakthrough in her life. Right when I said the word "breakthrough," the presence of God came over her, and she was slain in the Holy Spirit! Tonight was such an awesome experience, and I am excited this is just the beginning!

Chapter 2:
Be Careful What You Pray For

I've always loved the quote by Ellen Johnson Sirleaf: "If your dreams don't scare you they aren't big enough."

Growing up, I constantly asked God to give me big dreams and to use me to do big things for His kingdom. I remember being 15, on my knees, alone in my room, with God praying, "Lord, I do not want to be like everybody else! I do not want to live an ordinary life, but I want you to use my life to do extraordinary things for your kingdom! Speak to me. Use me. I want my life to be anything but average."

Going with the crowd or status quo has never been okay with me. Since a young age, I was always praying and dreaming of what God could do through me. I was constantly pursing God to give me vision for my life.

One of my big dreams was to attend college at Oral Roberts University. Growing up, I saw many people I knew went to ORU who were doing big things in the ministry. There, they made many great connections and met people who were helping them launch and run their ministries. Ever since the eighth grade, when I first heard about ORU, I dreamed about going there. Throughout high school, I worked hard with ORU as my end goal. Every time I did not want to do my homework or study for a test, I would think, No, you have to try hard or you won't be able to go to ORU!

I am happy to inform you that after some hard work, lots of prayer, and trust in God, I made it to ORU! I was enjoying my first semester as a college freshman. I was making a lot of new friends, finding things I could get involved in, and adjusting to living 16 plus hours away from my family, who was in Michigan. I felt like I was right where I needed to be, but I was not fully satisfied. And while I had continuously asked God to give me vision for my life and was studying at the university He had called me to attend, I thought it was time for me to start seeking the Lord on what the next step was in His plan for me.

During Christmas break, I began to focus my prayers. I took time to pray, fast, and to ask God what he wanted me to pursue and go after as we headed into the new year. If there's one thing I have learned in my walk with the Lord it is that when we pray and ask for God to give us something, he hears us, and he will deliver in his perfect timing. Also, you should be careful what you pray for! When you ask God to fill you with a big dream and vision, be ready, because our God is faithful, and He will give you one!

He did for me on January 3, 2012.

That afternoon, I was still home for Christmas break, and I had two days left in Michigan before I was to head back to ORU to start the second half of my freshman year. I was going about normal life (I was actually blow drying my hair) when God put a huge dream on my heart.

Some of you may be thinking that the moment God breathed a huge, new dream into my heart should have been a little more exciting than me standing in my parent's bathroom with the blow dryer in my hand, but I love exactly how that was the place and time God chose to speak to me. It proves God can speak to us anywhere and everywhere. We do not have to be kneeling at an alter or be out on the mission field for God to give us vision for our life. He can speak to us at any moment; we just have to be ready to listen.

While I was blow-drying my hair, God gave me a life-altering vision. I saw myself cutting a light purple ribbon. I saw young, dark skinned children running into a brand new house and jumping onto their brand new beds for the first time. In that moment, God spoke to me and said, "Kristie, I want you to start an orphanage."

After hearing that, I thought to myself, that makes sense. I've always wanted to start my own ministry, and I have a huge heart for orphans and children. Cool God! But, that was not all God wanted to say to me. Next he said, "And I want you to do this while you're still young. I want you to start to plan this and build this while you're in college." All of a sudden I wanted to take back the "Cool God!" comment because I felt completely overwhelmed! I actually laughed out loud and thought, Good one, God. That's not happening!

I remember this moment like it was yesterday. I sat at my desk chair in my bedroom to converse with God about this new idea. I thought, There is no way this is going to happen. First off, how do you even start an orphanage? I do not even know the first step I would take to get into something like that. They don't have a class at ORU called 'How to Start Your First Orphanage 101.' Next, orphanages aren't free. I don't have thousands of dollars in my bank account to pull something like this off, God. And finally, people will think I am absolutely crazy if I even say the idea out loud. Man, I even think this is absolutely crazy!

Then, God spoke to me and said, "People thought Noah was crazy when I asked him to build a big boat, and he saved all man-kind." He had me there! So I relented, "Okay God, I will do this for you, but you literally have to plop every last thing I need to do this right in my lap. I have no idea how to do this without you. Actually, I have no idea where to even start! If you plop every last thing I need right into my lap, I will do this."

Well, looks like I got the answer to what I was praying for. I was asking God to give me fresh vision and a new goal to work towards, and He answered. I did not really expect the vision to be quite as big as the first thing He asked of me to do though! After receiving the new vision and making up in my mind that I would do it, I did not tell a soul. I tried to completely forget about the vision. I figured it would eventually fade away if I did not mention it or think about it, and I would be off the hook.

I am sure you have probably assumed the vision did not just fade away. (This book would not exist if it had!) When

God gives you a vision for your life, it is not something you can simply forget or decide to go after with the little bit of extra time you have on your hands. It is something you need to take seriously and pursue.

Andy Stanley once said, "You have no idea what or who hangs in the balance of your decision to embrace the burden God has put on your heart." This is one of my favorite quotes when it comes to dealing with vision.

If you do not fully pursue and go after the vision God has given you for your life, you have no idea who is on the other side of it. You do not know who your lack of obedience will impact. When you choose to turn away from what God is calling you to do, lives hang in the balance. Where people spend eternity could hang in the balance. People may not know the Lord and life change might not occur because you failed to say "yes!" and embrace the burden God placed on your heart.

When I think of a person in the Bible who had a huge call from God and a burden on his heart for people, I think of Nehemiah. Nehemiah happens to be my favorite Bible character, and I think a lot of times his incredible story gets overlooked. Nehemiah had it made. He had a great job serving as the cupbearer to the King! He lived a very comfortable and satisfied life, but one day, God gave him a life altering call. While Nehemiah was living in his comfortable lifestyle, friends from Jerusalem (the city he was from) came and informed Nehemiah the people who still lived in Jerusalem were in trouble, the city was in horrible shape, and the wall of

Jerusalem had been broken down and burned with fire. In our society, walls do not have much meaning, but during this time, walls were as important as electricity or a police force. They symbolized strength and peace in a society. When Nehemiah heard that his people were in trouble, God put a burden on his heart. His heart was broken for his people and he fasted, prayed, and asked God for vision on what he should do next. God was calling Nehemiah to leave his position of comfort and status to rebuild the walls of Jerusalem and restore his city. Talk about an intimidating task!

Despite the challenges, obstacles, and hard times Nehemiah knew he would face, he chose to embrace the calling of God on his heart, and he left the place of security where he was to go after God's call on his life. Nehemiah understood a whole city and generation of people hung in the balance and would be lost if he said no to what God was calling him to do.

It is a long story, and I strongly encourage you to dive into the book of Nehemiah to read all the details of the story, but to sum it up quickly for you, God honored Nehemiah's obedience. He came through for him. He provided every last detail Nehemiah needed to complete his God-given task, and the city of Jerusalem was restored to its former glory all because one man chose to obey.

If God has put a big dream on your heart, I know how you feel. Trust me, I've been there. It's scary. It's overwhelming. It is way bigger than you. But, that is why it is called a God-sized dream. If it is a dream you can easily accomplish, you won't need to involve God in every part of it. You won't need to press into him when things get confusing. You won't grow in your faith as you watch God come through time and time again. God-sized dreams are supposed to go beyond yourself so you have no choice but to involve God in every aspect of the dream.

Take it from someone who has been there. If you have a God-sized dream, just say "Yes!" If you are praying for God to give you a God-sized vision for your life, believe me He will give it to you and when he does, say "Yes!"

You won't regret it. In fact, it will be an awesome ride, probably the best of your life. And, just like me, you will get to sit back and watch God plop every last thing you need to complete the task right into your lap.

Personal Journal Entry:

(A Prayer from my Prayer Journal)

June 22nd, 2012

Wow God, you never cease to amaze me! It's crazy God how you have every little detail of my life mapped out and under control. All along, You have been working in my life and fitting even the littlest details perfectly together, even when I could not see. I thank You for all the ways You have worked in my life, and I especially thank You for speaking to me and for putting many specific dreams and visions on my heart lately. I thank You for giving me a clear vision of what my future looks like and for giving me more specifics on what You have called me to do. God, I thank You in advance for the orphanage I will start in Haiti in the next few years. I thank you that things, which seem crazy and impossible to man, are made possible with You. God, I thank you in advance for all the orphans in Haiti that I will be able to rescue and place into the orphanage. God, I believe and trust that you will take care of and provide all the logistics. You will provide the connections in Haiti. You will provide the land in Haiti to build on. You will provide all the funds it will take to start this home. This task may seem crazy and impossible, but I thank You that You are my God, a God of miracles and with you, absolutely nothing is impossible. If You have called

me to do it, You will bring me through it! Let me keep my heart pure and my focus steady. Help me to not get distracted or discouraged by the things of this world. You are my rock, and in You I put my trust. I thank You I am never too young to do nation-shaking things for Your kingdom!
Amen.

Chapter 3:
Once, Okay. Twice... No Way.

After God places a big dream on a person heart, normal people tell someone or start planning their first move. Not me. I did not tell a soul. In fact, I wanted to forget the vision God had put on my heart. I kept convincing myself that it was probably just me coming up with a nice idea to help people, that it could not have been God, right?

After Christmas break was over, I went back to school to start the second half of my freshman year. I was focused on developing friendships, making memories, planning for the summer, normal things a freshman in college would be thinking about! But, that focus was not good enough for God.

One afternoon in late February, I was in the community bathroom on the floor of my dorm. As I was getting out of the shower, God gave me the exact same vision he showed me nearly a month and a half before. I saw myself opening an orphanage. I was cutting a light purple ribbon, and these little foreign children were running in to a brand new house, jumping onto their brand new beds for the first time. This time, God spoke to me saying, "Kristie, I want you to open an orphanage, and I want you to do this while you're young and in college. I want you to open it for around 20 kids in Haiti."

My reaction to the vision the second time around was much different from the first. The first time, I thought God had made a great joke, but this time, I was in shock and disbelief. As I stood there alone in the bathroom, tears began to well up in my eyes. I remember thinking, Wow, this is serious. That vision was not just a nice idea I had in my head. It is a call from God. I tried to forget about it, and He gave me that exact same vision again, with even more direction. Oh no, this is something He seriously wants me to pursue. I have to do this.

I went back to my dorm room and began researching facts about Haiti and orphans in the nation. I had never been to Haiti, and it was not really on my radar. I remember crying as I read the heart-wrenching statistics. One said that before the 2010 earthquake, there were around 300,000 orphans in the country but that since the earthquake, the number had doubled, and there was now an estimated 600,000 orphans in the nation. I also read that less than 50 percent of the kids in the country went to school and Haiti was the third hungriest nation in the world and the poorest in the Western Hemisphere. Little by little as I was reading about this nation, my heart was breaking. In that moment, I began to feel a heavy burden for these people, people I had never even met.

That afternoon, despite my fears and the many uncertainties that stood before me, I decided I had to at least attempt to go after this vision with everything in me. Why? Because the second time I had the vision was confirmation for me that it was the Lord's vision and plan, not my own.

In my mind, when God's calling me to do something, I have no choice but to fully run after it. I would hate to get to heaven, stand before God, and have Him say, "Kristie, thank you for reaching that group of girls, serving in your church, and for showing people my love. You did good, and you served me, but you missed what I called you to do. I created you to start a ministry and to open homes to rescue and change the lives of children who do not know me. That was my purpose and call for your life, and you missed it because you let your fears and doubts hold you back from obeying me. You were too afraid to take the risk. You missed it. But thank you for serving me. Come on in."

In my mind, that would be the worst welcome into heaven ever! I could never live with myself knowing the huge burden God had placed on my heart and knowing I turned the other way.

This morning, I was reading Exodus 3, where God revealed to Moses his call and purpose through a burning bush. Moses was also going about his daily business when a flaming bush that was not burning up caught his eye. He moved closer to the bush to check out the situation, and that's when God comes on the scene. God says to Moses:

> "I have indeed seen the misery of my people in Egypt. I have heard them crying out because of their slave drivers, and I am concerned about their suffering. So I

have come down to rescue them from the hand of the Egyptians and to bring them up out of that land into a good and spacious land, a land flowing with milk and honey—the home of the Canaanites, Hittites, Amorites, Perizzites, Hivites and Jebusites. And now the cry of the Israelites has reached me, and I have seen the way the Egyptians are oppressing them. So now, go. I am sending *YOU* to Pharaoh to bring my people the Israelites out of Egypt." But Moses said to God, "Who am I that I should go to Pharaoh and bring the Israelites out of Egypt?" And God said, "I will be with you. And this will be the sign to you that it is I who have sent you: When you have brought the people out of Egypt, you will worship God on this mountain."

Exodus 3:7-12 (NIV)

In the far side of the desert, on the Mountain of Horeb, through a burning bush, God chooses to get Moses' attention. God was calling Moses to bring the Israelites, His people, out of slavery, and from reading the passage above, we can see Moses was not 100 percent confident in what God was calling him to do. He is even quoted saying, "Who am I that I should go to Pharaoh and bring the Israelites out of Egypt?"

Moses thought he was just an ordinary guy, who was a part of a great family, helping his father-in-law look after his flock of sheep, but God had a different plan. On that mountaintop, God showed Moses he was called for something much greater. There, God was beginning to place a burden on his heart for the Israelites. A burden so deep, Moses knew he could not turn away from it despite his fears and uncertainties.

I am sure Moses felt the same way I did after he heard clear direction from the Lord. He probably felt confused, scared, and incapable, but I am also sure he knew what he heard God say was something he could not ignore. In the burning bush scene, God gave Moses his call. That is one of the many things I love about our God. He has a call for everyone, and He loves to reveal it to us in crazy ways. He may give it to you in the community bathroom of your dorm, or He may decide to set another bush on fire to get your attention! I do not know what God's got to do to get ahold of you, but I do know He has a purpose for your life. You simply have to ask Him what it is.

After hearing from the Lord to start a home while I was young and in college for a second time, I knew beyond the shadow of a doubt this was something God wanted me to do. After I finished sifting through all the sad statistics about the country of Haiti, I called my older sister, Shelby. I had to say it out loud to someone because, in my mind, once I tell someone I am going to do something, I fully intend to do it. I want to always be a woman whose actions match her words. Plus, my sister and I grew up being each others best friend (and still are), and she already knew how crazy I could be. So I figured she would not judge me!

I shared with Shelby the two different instances God had given me the vision and what He had told me to do each time. At the end of the story, I said, "I know it sounds crazy, so do not feel bad for telling me that it is. Even I think it is crazy!" After saying it out loud to another human being, the doubts began to creep back into my mind, and I started thinking about how unreal and impractical this whole thing was. What my sister said to me next changed my perspective. She said, "Kristie, I don't think this is crazy. You have known since a very young age that God has called you to be a missionary, and you have always dreamed of starting your own ministry. To me, it seems like God is just revealing to you His next step for your life. The timing actually makes perfect sense to me."

I am so thankful for a sister who believed in me when I did not even believe in myself. What Shelby said was exactly right. Throughout my young life and teenage years, I had daydreamed and pictured countless times what it would be like to have a ministry just like the one God was revealing to me. One that helped the least of these. One that reached people and spoke for people who could not speak for themselves. One that pointed people to Jesus. This new vision God had given me over those few months was His way of showing me how to get there. Now that I had received clear direction, the question became: Would I start going after it, or would I be too scared and let my fear overtake my courage? Would I have enough faith to completely let go and say "yes" to what God was calling me to do?

Saying "yes" to God is definitely something easier said than done. That three-letter word is easy to say, but to actually carry out what you have said "yes" to is the hard part.

I know one thing, everything inside you changes when you say "yes" to the burden God has put on your heart. It's as if your eyes have been opened for the first time. When you say "yes" to God, He ignites a fire, a passion in your heart for something you never knew you had before.

Mother Teresa, one of the most inspirational women to walk the planet, said it best: "We must know exactly when we say 'yes' to God what is in that '*yes.*' *Yes* means 'I surrender,' totally, fully, without any counting the cost, without any examination: 'Is it all right? Is it convenient?' Our 'yes' to God is without any reservations. It's nothing but a single word: 'Yes! I accept whatever you give, and I give whatever you take.' It doesn't mean extraordinary things, understanding big things—it is a simple acceptance, because I have given myself to God, because I belong to him."

That afternoon, I chose to say "Yes!" I decided I was going to pursue the vision God had laid on my heart with everything in me. I was not sure how it was going to go or how it was even going to start, but I did know that I had to be obedient to what God was calling me to do. If I did not go after it, I would have to live the rest of my life knowing I did not have the courage to go after what God wanted me to do. I would have to live knowing I said "no" because I was too afraid.

Let me encourage you to always follow what the Lord is saying and to let your faith outweigh your fear. And let me just tell you—when you say "yes" to God, you better buckle up! It's about to be one heck of a ride.

Personal Journal Entry from Prayer Journal:

November 17, 2013

Father God,

I love You, and I thank You for the big vision You have given me to start an orphanage in Haiti. It is such a beautiful dream, but at the same time, it is a task that is way beyond me. But, I thank You that nothing is too big for You, my God. Help me focus on the next steps, and help me remember to take it day by day. Instead of focusing on this "mountain" of a dream I have to climb, continue to give me the next steps, and continue to open doors little by little until it is accomplished. I trust You with this, God, and I thank You for already working out every little detail. Continue to grow the plan, and give me fresh revelation from You. This is all for you . . . Thank you for choosing my hands and my heart to work through. Please continue to piece every little detail together. I thank you for seeing my timeline and for bringing everything to pass in your perfect timing. I thank you for placing such great people in my life who are going to come alongside me and help me. Continue to place people in my life who will speak into me and encourage me.

    I thank you I can do this through you, who is constantly giving me strength.

    Amen.

Chapter 4:
Get Up & Go.

After saying "yes" to such a big dream, you might be wondering, Where does one even begin? Good question. I was thought the exact same thing, when God first gave me the vision for the orphanage.

I decided I should probably go to Haiti at least once before moving forward on starting an orphanage there. After all, I had never been to Haiti, and I had never had the desire to go there. But after researching and learning a little about the nation, I knew I could not just sit back and do nothing. I felt so uncomfortable going through the motions of my normal life while I knew there were children sleeping on the streets each night, without food, water, and a family who loved them, and God was calling me to do something about it. I knew I had to act—God had put a burden for them on my heart.

ORU was sending a missions team to Haiti for two weeks that coming summer, and I signed up for the trip. Even though I did not really know how to get this vision up and running, I thought going to Haiti was the logical first step. Over the years, I have learned that is exactly what you need to do when you have a God given dream. Start with what you have and what you know to do. Take it step by step. If you look at the whole picture and think of everything you have to accomplish to get from start to finish, I guarantee you will feel overwhelmed. When God puts a dream on your heart, He purposefully does not give you the whole picture. If he did, you would see all the obstacles and difficult times standing in your way of making it to the finish line, and you would likely bow out.

Abraham had one of the biggest calling of God on his life. God called him to be the father of many nations. That is no small task!

> But Abram said, "Sovereign Lord, what can you give me since I remain childless and the one who will inherit my estate is Eliezer of Damascus?" And Abram said, "You have given me no children; so a servant in my household will be my heir." Then the word of the Lord came to him: "This man will not be your heir, but a son who is your own flesh and blood will be your heir." He took him outside and said, "Look up at the sky and count the stars—if indeed you can count them." Then he said to him, "So shall your offspring be."
>
> Genesis 15:2-5 (NIV)

When Abraham initially heard God calling him to be the father of many nations, he definitely did not know all of the difficulties that would surround this calling. God did not show him that Sarai, his wife, would not be able to get pregnant, and she would not have their first child until she was 90 years old. He did not show Abraham all the family drama that would go down between him, Sarai, Hagar, Ishmael, and Isaac. God did not show Abraham that He was going to tell him to sacrifice and almost kill his only son, Isaac, whom he waited so long for. If God would have revealed all the difficult moments of the journey to Abraham in the beginning, I doubt he would have even started. God purposefully gives us a small picture of what He is calling us to do in the beginning stages. He is then counting on us to say "yes" to His call and to start taking our first steps of faith based on what we know to do. When God sees us taking small steps of faith forward and trusting in Him in things we cannot see, He will honor that, and He will move mountains in order to make His dream for your life a reality.

When you have a call of God on your life, you need to take a moment and say, "Okay God, what can I do today? What can I do right now, in this season of my life, to start to pursue this call?" And then get up, go, and start doing it.

In that season of my life, all I knew to do was go to Haiti to explore the possibility of starting this home. Once I was officially signed up, I thought God will surely open up the next door or show me what the next step was on this trip. I was sure He would give me some kind of sign or further direction confirming Haiti was the place I was supposed to open this orphanage. I assumed I would be holding an orphan and God would shout down from the heavens, "This is the place, Kristie! Start this home here!" You may be shocked to read this, but unfortunately, that did not happen. But, this first trip to Haiti was a pivotal and necessary part of my journey to starting the orphanage.

Throughout the two weeks of our trip, we visited many different orphanages. There was one orphanage we visited several times throughout our trip, and it really stood out to me. This home was called Eve Rose's Orphanage, and she had around 20 children living there. Eve Rose was a Haitian woman who grew up in Haiti, went to school in the United States, and then moved back to Haiti to start this orphanage. The way Eve Rose was raising and taking care of her children was incredible. She was full of joy and life and so were all of the children in her home. These kids were so sweet and so much fun to spend time with, but beyond that, every child had a deep, genuine, and real relationship with Jesus Christ. This group of kids truly knew the Lord, and it was very evident they had strong relationships with their Savior just from the few days we were visiting them. Every day, these children would have intense worship and prayer sessions. They would worship God with hands raised and eyes closed with tears flowing through the corners. They had such a hunger to seek the Lord, and most of these kids were only 6, 7, and 8 years old!

On the last day of our visit, when my team was saying goodbye and preparing to leave, each little child came around our missions team and laid hands on us! It was incredible to see these young kids lifting us, the missionaries, up in prayer… and man, they were powerful prayers! As our team pulled away in our truck, waving to the kids as we went, I knew in that moment I would never forget that home or those children. Eve Rose's Orphanage had marked my heart.

Another essential moment during my first trip to Haiti happened during a team prayer night. It was a beautiful summer night, and our team was gathered outside to pray. In the middle of the prayer session, our team leader encouraged us to ask the Lord to give us a word for someone else on the team and then to speak it to them and pray over them. I began to pray for God to give me a word for someone, and I felt him whispering to my heart, "Go pray for Hannah." I thought Okay, will do, but what am I praying for? Can you give me a little more here, God? He did not tell me anything to pray for, but He just kept putting on my heart to go pray for her. I got up, walked over to Hannah, and asked her if I could pray for her. She of course said "yes," and I began to pray a pretty basic and general prayer over her life since God had not given me any specifics. After I was through with my prayer, she looked at me and said, "Wow Kristie, it is crazy that you came over here asking to pray for me because this whole time we've been sitting here praying, God has been putting on my heart so many things I need to tell you." Now it made sense why God kept telling me to go pray for Hannah.

Before I get into what Hannah told me, let me give you a little background on our relationship. Hannah and I were not best friends or anything. We knew each other from ORU and had previously met through a mutual friend. I really did not know her anymore than saying "Hi, how are you?" when we passed each other on the sidewalk at school. Hannah was an awesome girl, but we were just starting to develop a relationship on the mission trip, and she did not know a lot about me. I do not even think she knew that full time missions was what I wanted to do with my life, and she definitely had no idea that God gave me a vision to start an orphanage in Haiti and how I was on the trip to look for an answer to that vision. Now that you know all this, the next part will probably be bizarre, and you will know how it was truly God speaking through her to me that night.

She said, "Kristie, I was reading Jeremiah 1 and I feel like the Lord is wanting me to tell you this is your chapter." She read to me Jeremiah 1:4-10, which says:

> The word of the Lord came to me, saying, "Before I formed you in the womb I knew you, before you were born I set you apart; I appointed you as a prophet to the nations."
>
> "Alas, Sovereign Lord," I said, "I do not know how to speak; I am too young." But the Lord said to me, "Do not say, 'I am too young.' You must go to everyone I send you to and say whatever I command you. Do not be afraid of them, for I am with you and will rescue you," declares the Lord.
>
> Then the Lord reached out his hand and touched my mouth and said to me, "I have put my words in your mouth. See, today I appoint you over nations and kingdoms to uproot and tear down, to destroy and overthrow, to build and to plant."

After reading this, Hannah said, "Just like the Lord called Jeremiah to go to the nations, He is calling you too. I feel that God wants me to tell you that you are not too young or inexperienced to start to go after the huge dream that God has put on your heart. He has given you the tools. He has called you, and He has equipped you for the task. You may not think you're ready or you may think you are too young to carry out such a big task, just like Jeremiah, but you are not. God has called you for such a time as this, and you should not be afraid because God is with you. You do not need to worry about anything because God will provide for you, just as He provided the words for Jeremiah to speak, He will give you what you need."

I was silent, hanging onto every word that Hannah (or the Lord really) was saying. She went on to say, "Also, I feel like God wants me to tell you that you do not need a man to start going after the dreams that God has put on your heart. It is your heart that God has put the dream in. You are the one who is equipped. He has called you to do it, and He has given you the necessary tools to get it done. You do not need a man to get started. This is God's dream for your life."

I was absolutely blown away. This word was straight from God because it was exactly what I needed to hear, and I was so thankful that Hannah was obedient in communicating it to me!

Here are three thoughts I immediately had after Hannah finished speaking to me:

1. It's crazy God gave her Jeremiah 1. The section she read has always been one of my favorite passages of scripture, and Jeremiah has always been one of my favorite Bible characters. I always have identified myself with Jeremiah because he is someone who God gave a huge calling to at a young age, and he was intimidated by his age. I am so thankful that age is just a number to God. Growing up, I always prayed I could be like Jeremiah. I wanted God to use me to do big things for His kingdom while I was young, just like he used Jeremiah.

2. It's crazy Hannah kept saying, "This big dream that God has given you," when she had no clue about the vision of the orphanage. She kept saying that God would be with me and that He would provide for this huge calling, when she had no idea what God would be providing for.

3. It's crazy God told Hannah He prepared me to do this by myself, and I did not need a man in order to accomplish this dream. Up until that point, I had always thought that once I find my husband, we can start a ministry together, travel the world giving people Jesus, and we would basically be the next John and Lisa Bevere. I had all these big ministry dreams on my heart, but I could not start them until I was married.

As I am writing this now, I laugh thinking that is how I thought my life would go. God obviously wanted me to take a different path! When Hannah said this, I realized that she (or God) was right! What was I waiting for? This was my dream, which God had put on my heart. God had given this vision to me with the intent that I would carry it out.

As humans, we tend to make up excuses, which often hold us back. We say to ourselves, "Your plan sounds great, God! As soon as I get my significant other, a million dollars, done with school, four kids, etc, I will begin to move and go after what You are calling me to do."

Jeremiah made up excuses too. He told God he could not possibly be the man whom God would move through because he was too young and he did not know what to say. We can see from the passage above in Jeremiah 1, God does not put up with excuses. He told Jeremiah he was not too young and He would provide the words for him. The truth is, there will always be a new excuse we can come up with. I had a lot: I do not know how to do this. I am only 18. I am no where close to getting married, to name a few! But, God is bigger than the excuses or any limit we try to put on ourselves. When God is looking for a person to use He does not look at all their limiting factors, He looks for a person who has a willing and obedient heart. Those are the ingredients God needs to use an ordinary life to do a extraordinary thing for His kingdom.

After Hannah shared that word with me, I said, "Hannah if you only knew the weight of the words that you just said. That was straight from the Lord because it was exactly what I needed to hear!" I shared with her the whole story and told her all about the vision that God had given me to start the orphanage in Haiti. I am so thankful for people who listen to the Lord, like Hannah. Thank God Hannah was not too intimidated to share what the Lord was telling her to say to me. If she had been, who knows where I would be! Her word from the Lord confirmed that I had heard from God, I was not "crazy," and I was on the right path to following my God given dream.

Before I knew it, the two weeks in Haiti were through, and we were on our plane back to the US. Pretty sure that everyone on the plane was sleeping but me. I was up reflecting on the week. I remember sitting on the plane, praying silently, "Lord, this was such a great trip, but I feel I did not get the answer I needed. I needed confirmation Haiti is the place you want me to open this home. I needed you to open a huge door or to clearly show me the next step, and I still feel like I am back at square one, unsure of where to go from here." As I was praying, God spoke to me and said, "Kristie, think of all of the children in Eve Rose's orphanage. They know Me, and they are falling more in love with Me every day. They are going to grow up and become leaders in the nation of Haiti. They have so much potential. Now, think of all the other children who are in Haiti, living on the streets, who could have the same amount of potential but have nothing because no one has rescued them. I want you to go back and rescue them."

That was all the confirmation I needed. Haiti was the place where the orphanage would open. The journey had only just begun.

Personal Journal Entry:

May 21st, 2012

(Written on 2012 trip to Haiti)

Today, we spent the entire morning at Eve Roses's orphanage hanging out with all of her precious children. It was so fun! I got to spend time with my buddy Anso again, and I also made two new friends—brothers named Falin and Malin. I played soccer with the kids and gave them some little toys, which they loved! It is evident these children have Christ in their hearts. I can see that just from the way they treat us and how they treat each other. The kids are so joyful and loving, regardless of the circumstances they live in. Spending time at Eve Rose's has definitely been my favorite part of the trip, and I will remember these kids forever!

Tonight, our team had a time of worship and prayer. We prayed for team members who we felt God had given us a word for. God did not necessarily give me a specific word for my friend Hannah, but I felt Him leading me to pray for her. I went over and prayed a general prayer of encouragement over her. After I was done praying, she told me how weird it was I came over to her because God had given her some encouraging things and a word to say to me. She explained she was kind of timid to tell me because she did not think I needed it because I always seemed so joyful! Haha! I explained to her how I always could use some encouragement!

It was totally worth the Lord sending me over to her because everything she said was completely what I needed to hear! Hannah told me as she was reading Jeremiah 1 the Lord put me on her heart and told her it was for me. She told me God was going to use me, like Jeremiah, as a prophet to the nations. She told me to not be intimated by the big dream God had put on my heart, but to boldly go after it. She also told me that I did not need a man to start my ministry. Hannah said God had made me powerful and strong enough to carry out the vision. He had equipped me to go to the nations and to preach the Gospel.... It was my call. When Hannah said this, it was such a word of confirmation for me. I felt like God has been speaking that to me this past year, and it was so awesome to hear it spoken from God, through someone else. All the words she spoke to me are confirmation I am on the right track. God has my whole life in his hands, and He will set every connection up for me. I just have to wait on his timing, seek Him, and press into Him hard in the meantime. I was so encouraged, grateful, and thankful for the words Hannah shared with me.

Chapter 5:
Prep Time

"Vision is a clear mental picture of what could be, fueled by the conviction that it should be. Anyone with a vision will tell you this is not merely something that could be done. This is something that should be done. This is something that must happen."

-Andy Stanley, *Visioneering*

After I returned from Haiti, I felt so compelled to act. I knew beyond the shadow of a doubt I was supposed to open a home in Haiti. I felt so impressed to move forward on the dream God had given me. Even though I was overwhelmed and did not quite know where to begin, I had received the confirmation I needed, and I was all in.

First, I prayed a lot. I did not know what to do next except to pray and to ask God to start opening doors. When you have a God given dream, praying about it is the best place to start. When we pray for our dreams, we are involving God. We are starting off by saying "God, I want You in the picture. I want You involved in every part of this journey. I know I cannot do it without You, and You will be the one who receives all the glory once I reach the destination."

When I think of a man who took the right steps when reaching his God given dream, again I think of Nehemiah. He involved prayer first on his journey to accomplishing the vision God put on his heart. Nehemiah was called to rebuild the city wall and to restore the city of Jerusalem. There was four months between the time he initially heard the call from God and the time he was actually in the right place to start making moves forward on the plan. During those four months, Nehemiah did not sit around waiting for the time when he could take action. He was very active during a season that people from the outside looking in may have considered to be inactive. During those four months, Nehemiah prayed and asked God for direction. He planned his course, and he let God guide and build the vision inside of his heart.

By the time the four months were up and Nehemiah was granted permission to leave his job serving the King to pursue his calling, he already had his plan in place. He knew what his next moves would be because he was intentional about seeking God, strategizing, planning, and preparing for the time to take action. Nehemiah allowed time for God to hammer out the vision in his heart and to give him clear direction.

Those seasons of so-called "inactivity" are actually very important and crucial for a person with a God given vision. The years following my trip to Haiti in 2012 was the time

I allowed for God to direct me, speak to me, and show me exactly what He wanted the home to look like. I did not tell many people about the vision during these few years. In fact, I probably do not even need both hands to count the number of people who knew about what the Lord had laid on my heart to do. It was not the season to share what God was doing, but it was the season to pray, plan, and prepare for what was coming.

During that season, God gave me so much! I would pray and think about the orphanage all the time. I would pray and think about it during my quiet time, in the shower, while I was working, every jog around my neighborhood. The orphanage was constantly on my mind. God would speak to me and give me direction during the most unusual and random times. I remember one afternoon, I was planting flowers in my backyard, and God showed me a clear vision of what the home was supposed to look like. Tears began to well up in my eyes. Things were getting real. That night, I drew a sketch of what God had shown me. Another time, I was running on the track around the baseball field at my school, and God showed me faces of young kids, smiling, laughing, and playing together. That definitely motivated me to run faster.

God also gave me the name for the ministry and the home during that season. I have always loved Mark 10:14, which says, "When Jesus saw this, he was indignant. He said to them, 'Let the little children come to me, and do not hinder them, for the kingdom of God belongs to such as these'" (NIV). This verse displays God's love for children and how He sees unlimited potential in them, even when people do not. Here, Jesus recognizes kids are just as important as any other believer, and they too can be used to do big things for his Kingdom, even though they are young.

The name came from this verse. God showed me that he wanted me to start a home where kids could learn about the Lord and where they could fully understand what it means to truly know God. Then, he showed me to teach these kids how to go out and reach others for Jesus. The mission of our ministry is to bring children into the Kingdom of God and to disciple and train them how to do ministry and how to bring others into the Kingdom of God. He showed me that they would be Kingdom Kids.

And there was the name: Kingdom Kids Home.

During this season, God also gave me ideas and inspiration of what we were supposed to teach our kids at Kingdom Kids Home. I remember one day, I was sitting in one of my theology classes at ORU and we were watching a video called, "Fingerprint of God." During this video, they spotlighted Heidi Baker's children's ministry over in Africa. While I was watching this spotlight on her children's ministry, I was amazed at what I was seeing. The children in her ministry we ministering to other people. The kids were speaking, leading worship, and praying for people. While I was watching this, God started speaking to me. I quickly grabbed my notebook and wrote down what He was saying. Here's what I wrote down:

October 10th, 2013

I am calling you to the nations and to show children My glory. "How will they know if they do not hear?" You need to go and tell them of My goodness and share with them the love I have for them. I am calling you to teach them how to love others truly and deeply, a love modeled after My own. You need to teach them what it means to care for one another. You will be their example. They will see how you love Me and others, and they will be inspired to love in the same way. Teach them how to share Jesus with people. Teach them how to have a heart of worship. Teach them how to lay hands on one another to see healing. For they will be the next generation of leaders to rise up and see change in their nation. Then, in turn, they will pour out God's love on their nation and other nations of the world.

God was continuing to grow and expand the vision. In that class, God told me to teach the kids of Kingdom Kids Home how to do hands on ministry. To teach them, use them, and show them what it looks like to do big things for God's Kingdom while they were growing up in the home. This way, by the time they grow up and leave the home, a heart of ministry will be so engraved in each of them that they will not be able to help but take it everywhere they go.

Another moment where God gave me clear direction of something I needed to implement in the future Kingdom

Kids Home happened during a chapel service my sophomore year at ORU. Our university president, Dr. Mark Rutland, was preaching a message on dreams. He told a story I will never forget. When he was in fifth grade, his teacher would sit her students on the carpet of her classroom, and they would have "Dream Day." The teacher would go around as ask each child what their dream was. Once they shared their dream, she would take that dream and speak life into it. For example, when Dr. Rutland was asked what his dream was, he told his teacher he wanted to be an author. His teacher said something along the lines of, "Wow! You are going to be such a great author! I cannot wait till I go to the bookstore years from now and I see your book sitting on the shelf. I am going to pick it up and tell everyone at the store, 'This was my fifth grade student! Buy his book!'" Dr. Rutland said after his teacher's encouragement, he felt as if he could write a hundred best selling books. This teacher encouraged her students' dreams and made them feel like they could do anything they put their minds to ... and it worked for Dr. Rutland! He now has 15 books on the New York's Times best-selling author list!

As Dr. Rutland shared this story, God spoke to me and said, "Kristie, that's what I want you to do at Kingdom Kids Home. I want you to encourage the kids to dream God-sized dreams and tell them they are never too young to start going after the dreams I will put on their hearts." After that, it was official! "Dream Day" would be something we would do very often at Kingdom Kids Home.

Even though this part in the journey was not the most glamorous or miraculous time, it was a crucial time. This season of praying, planning, and preparing ended up being about a year and a half. I am so thankful for this season where God gave me clear direction. This way, when doors opened and it came time to act, I did not have to stop and think about how things would be or how we should set things up because God had already given all of it to me during my time of praying and waiting.

If God has given you a vision and you are ready to take action, I know how you feel. I have definitely been there. Personally, I am not very patient (I'm working on that), and I do not like waiting around. But, before you start making moves, have you prayed about the vision? Have you taken the time to let God give you clear direction? Have you made time for him to hammer out the vision in your heart? If you have not, I strongly encourage you start doing those things! That is the best first step to getting on the right road to following your God-given dream. It worked for Nehemiah. It worked for me. I know it can work for you.

> But seek first His kingdom and His righteousness, and all these things will be given to you as well.
>
> Matthew 6:33 (NIV)

Personal Journal Entry:

June 18th, 2012

After returning from Haiti, the country and all those precious children are what consume most of my thoughts these days. I actually cannot stop thinking about it. I know beyond the shadow of a doubt God is calling me to return to Haiti to start an orphanage within the next few years. I have known for about six months now that God has called me to start an orphanage for about 20 children, and now, I am certain Haiti is the place where the Lord wants it to happen. I am so excited for this! It's seriously all I can think about lately! I do not think I have ever wanted anything more! I even wished for this when I blew out the candles on my 19th birthday two weeks ago, haha! Right now, this summer, I am praying that God will continue to build up this dream in my heart and for Him to give me more insight about how I am supposed to do this. There are so many kids on the streets, on their own down there, who will never have the potential to become anything unless they are rescued … and that is exactly what I intend to do.

Chapter 6:
Not A Cake Walk

I wish I could tell you the journey to starting Kingdom Kids Homes was all fun and games. Up to this point, the path seemed fairly simple. God gave me a dream, I said "I'm in," and I began traveling on the road to the destination. I wish I could say it was that easy … but since when has obeying God ever been easy?

After I returned from my first trip to Haiti in 2012, I was all in. As I mentioned before, I did not have a clue how I would start an orphanage in Haiti, but I did know it was what God was calling me to do and I had to do everything in my power to make it happen. That summer, I started with what I knew. I spoke with a friend who had close friends who were full time missionaries in Haiti, and he suggested I share my vision with them. I thought that was a great idea, and it seemed like the most logical first step. I told my friend to inform the missionaries about me, what I felt God was calling me to do, and to see if I could have a Skype meeting with them. This was me putting myself out there and attempting to take a small step toward a big dream. About a week after I took that first, small step, the enemy decided to throw an obstacle my way.

Nearly a month and a half after I returned from Haiti, my whole family went on a vacation to the beautiful island of Hawaii. One day, we were out on a four-hour boating and snorkeling excursion. It was a perfect day, and we were swimming right next to giant sea turtles. While we were snorkeling at our first stop, my stomach started to hurt. I swam back to the boat and as I climbed on board I started to experience very intense pain in my stomach. The pain continued to get worse, and it felt as if someone was stabbing me with a sword right above my right hip. For the remainder of the excursion, which was about three more hours, I laid on my mom's lap in excruciating pain, confused to what was going on. I had never felt such a sharp pain before.

As soon as we got back to shore, I hurried back to our hotel room because all I wanted to do was lie down in a bed after rocking in a boat for three miserable hours. Back in the room, I would pace the floor, lay in the bed, and sit in a chair trying to find a comfortable position where I would not experience the sharp pain, but none of that helped. The pain would not leave—no matter what position I was in. After being in pain for about four more hours, we decided to go to the urgent care at the hotel next door.

Right when the doctor saw me, he took a look at my stomach and said "Wow, your stomach is so swollen and huge. This is not normal!" He sent me to the emergency room right away.

My parents drove me to the hospital, which was on the other side of the island of Maui. We arrived around ten at night and once admitted to my room, I was told that I had passed a kidney stone. That explained the excruciating pain I had been in for the previous ten hours! Then, the doctor informed us something else was wrong. I either had a pelvic mass or a massive cyst on the inside of me. What?

The doctor said if it was a pelvic mass they would have to perform emergency surgery that night, but if it was a cystic mass, I would be safe to go home and have a scheduled surgery. After several more tests, some that were very painful, the doctors told me I had a cystic mass the size of a football in my stomach, and they had never seen one that big before. The cyst was the size of a baby that was 6lbs . . . and yes, I did look a little pregnant. After a long night in Maui's hospital, the doctors released me around five in the morning.

I finished the next few days in Hawaii, and we headed back home where I would have the cyst removed within the next two weeks. The Sunday morning before my surgery, my mom and I went to my pastor's wife for prayer before I went into surgery. After she was done praying for me, my pastor's wife said, "The whole time I was praying for you, I just felt in my spirit this whole sickness is an attack of the devil. He is trying to stop you and slow you down. I do not know why, but I feel this whole thing is the enemy trying to bring you down."

I could not have agreed with her more. I knew exactly why the devil was attacking me. It was no coincidence that this whole sickness was brought on right when I took my first, small step towards a great big dream. The doctors said this cyst had been growing in me for months now. It appears that as God was forming the dream of Kingdom Kids Homes in my heart, the devil was also forming his own plan of attack for me. He was trying to put up whatever resistance and obstacles he could to get me off course from following God's plan. But what the devil did not know, was that I would take on quite a few more cysts and major surgeries before I would abandon the dream that God had planted in my heart. "Though the righteous fall seven times, they rise again" (Proverbs 24:16). I knew God was on my side, so there was no need to be afraid of the devil's schemes.

My surgery was supposed to be a quick, one-hour, outpatient surgery. After the surgery, I would recover in the hospital for about an hour, and then I would head home. When I woke up from my surgery and saw my mom, she informed me my surgery had some complications. Instead of a one-hour surgery, it ended up being four and a half hours. The doctors thought the cyst was on my ovary, but once they got a look inside they saw that it was higher up and surrounded by blood vessels and arteries that led to my heart. They had to be extremely careful when they were removing the cyst because if they had cut one of vessels to my heart, I would probably not be writing this right now. I am very thankful for doctors with steady hands and for God watching over me throughout the surgery.

Since my surgery had some complications, I ended up staying in the hospital for a night so the doctors could make sure I was not bleeding internally.

As I lay alone in my hospital room that night, I remember reading Psalm 27 (NIV) and focusing in on verses 1, 2, and 13. Even today, this is still my favorite Psalm. Those verses said:

> The Lord is my light and my salvation—whom shall I fear? The Lord is the stronghold of my life—whom shall I be afraid? When the wicked advance against me to devour me, it is my enemies and my foes who will stumble and fall. . . . I will remain confident in this: I will see the goodness of the Lord in the land of the living.

That last verse quickly became the cry of my heart for the entire journey of launching Kingdom Kids Homes. Through the toughest and most discouraging times, I would say to myself: "Despite the challenges I am facing, I will remain confident in this—I will see the goodness of the Lord."

Surprisingly, I am thankful the journey has not been easy. In times of trouble and in circumstances our human hands cannot control, you realize your need for a Savior and you learn how to trust God in the midst of confusion. Just look at Joseph. God has given us the perfect example of someone who went through confusion and hardship on the path to his God-give dreams.

God began giving Joseph dreams at a young age. He had ten older brothers, and God gave Joseph a dream where he saw all of his older brothers bowing down to him. Joseph knew from a young age he was destined to rule. His brothers did not like the sound of that, and they sold Joseph into slavery.

Talk about a rough time! I am sure Joseph was confused while working as a slave, since God had originally showed him though his dreams that he would be the one ruling and in charge. But, even when Joseph was not where he wanted to be, he still trusted God, gave it his all, and served his master, Potiphar, with excellence. Just as things started going well while Joseph was working as a slave, Potiphar's wife lied about Joseph, and he was thrown into prison. I am sure Joseph probably thought he was on a major detour and not on track to get to the throne any time soon.

I think it is safe to say prison was a "desert" type season for Joseph. He was probably discouraged, wondering why he was spending time in a prison cell when God had called him to rule. But little did he know, God still had his hand on Joseph's life. He was developing Joseph in his desert season and preparing him for his time as a ruler. While Joseph was in the "desert," God was teaching Joseph how to trust in him, even in the midst of confusion and hard times.

Just like He did with Joseph, God uses hard circumstances to shape us into the person He is calling us to be. The journey is not supposed to be easy. In hard seasons, our character is developed. In tough times, we learn what it looks like to press into God. When things do not go the way we planned, we recognize our need for Him. That way, when you reach your mountaintop and arrive at your destination, you'll look back on all you endured and you will know God is the one who carried you there and who saw you through your troubles.

Joseph was faithful to the Lord despite his circumstances, and God honored him because of it. He found himself as second in command in all Egypt, and he saved the country from years of famine. I love the story of Joseph because it shows us God always has a plan for our lives. In times of hardship, we need to remember the Word of God says, "I will guide you along the best pathway for your life. I will advise you and watch over you" (Psalm 32:8, NIV). God always has our lives in the palm of His hand. Even in the hard seasons, He is always right there with us.

I'm thankful the journey to building Kingdom Kids Home was not a cake walk because as the challenges grew, so did my faith. If Joseph were here today, I am sure he would tell you that going after a God given dream is not always easy, but it is completely worth it . . . and on that fact, I would have to agree with him.

Personal Journal Entry from My Prayer Journal:

July 16th, 2012
My beautiful Jesus,
God, You never cease to amaze me. I love You more than my words could express. Your love and how You constantly have my life in your hands continues to amaze me. God, I thank You the devil does not even have a foothold in my life in the name of Jesus. I command every attack of the enemy to flee in Jesus name. I thank You that tomorrow, during my surgery, You will be guiding the doctors' hands and their every move. Jesus, I belong to you. You hold my world in your hands, and I completely trust You with it.

*You are a good God. I thank you in advance for a complication-free surgery and a quick recovery time. I know You have an incredible plan and destiny in store for me. No matter what obstacles or opposition the enemy tries to throw at me, I will never stop serving You, loving You, praising You, and living out all of the God-given dreams You have placed on my heart. So, bring it on, devil! I will **never** waver from my God. Give me Your strength, Jesus, to stand against the devil. I love You, and I commit my entire being to You. You are everything to me. I thank You for all the God-sized dreams You have been placing on my heart, and I trust and believe You are already opening the doors and paving the way for every last one of them to come true!*

Amen.

Chapter 7:
Too Late To Turn Back Now

If it had been up to me, I would have headed back to Haiti in the summer of 2013. I didn't want to wait around. I was ready to full-on pursue my God given vision. When I prayed about when I should go back and who I should go with, the answer God gave me was surprising. He told me that He did not want me to go back to Haiti in 2013 at all, but instead, he wanted me to pray and prepare that summer. After hearing this, I was pretty sure I had heard wrong. I did not want to delay it another year. In my mind, I already knew what I wanted to do, so what was there to plan for?

I remember it like it was yesterday. I was driving in my car thinking about this and God told me, "Kristie, you are not going back to Haiti this summer because I want you to plan, prepare, and pray for the dream. You will go back in the summer of 2014 to find the home and make the plans. Then, you will open the home after you graduate college in summer 2015." I was slightly annoyed by hearing this because I was ready to go, but then I remembered God knows best and has perfect timing, so I submitted to Him.

If you have ever read the Bible, you most likely know the highlights of David's life. Everyone talks about David being anointed King, defeating Goliath, and reigning as King of Israel. Most people fail to realize how long David had to wait between all these significant events. David was anointed king at 15 years old, but did not actually have the crown until he was 30. I do not know about you, but 15 years is an extremely long time to wait in my mind! Not to mention, the 15 years David was waiting on the Lord to fulfill His promise was not the easiest and calmest time of David's young life—in fact, it was probably the most difficult period. David spent most of those years running for his life!

Once Saul, the current king of Israel, realized David was next in line for the crown and once he saw how much the people loved David, he became very jealous and wanted to take David's life. David spent most of his years of waiting hiding out in caves and looking over his shoulder everywhere he went. I did not know David personally, but I am guessing this is far from what David imagined his life would be like leading up to the throne.

Even though those years were hard and not ideal for David, they were so essential to his story. God taught David and shaped him into the man and leader he was called to be during his years of hiding. God was taking David through a season of brokenness, where his comfort, security, position, and title were stripped away from him for a season, and he had to learn how to lean on, trust in, and seek after God.

There was a time during this season where David had the chance to cut short his season of brokenness. David was hiding out in a cave when King Saul walked in to go to the bathroom. King Saul had no idea David and his men were hiding in there. David's men told David to kill King Saul. They knew if King Saul was dead, all the running around and hiding would be over and David would finally get to be king! David sneaked up on King Saul, but only cut off a corner of his robe. He did not kill him. He came back to his men and gave them an explanation.

> "The Lord forbid that I should do such a thing to my master, the Lord's anointed, or lay my hand on him; for he is the anointed of the Lord." With these words David sharply rebuked his men and did not allow them to attack Saul. And Saul left the cave and went his way.
>
> 1 Samuel 24:6-7, NIV

The verses above reveal David's level of trust in God's plan. Even though David would have loved for his time of running to be over, he knew it was God's plan for Saul to be King during that time. He recognized Saul was the Lord's anointed for that time, and he would be manipulating God's plan and God's will for his life if he would have taken King Saul's life. Even though David's life would have immediately become a lot easier, he chose to wait, rest in God's promise, and let God's will play out. He realized God was shaping him, teaching him, and making him into the man He called him to be during this season of brokenness, and he did not want to end prematurely what God was teaching him in his life. He trusted God's promise would be fulfilled in God's perfect way and in God's perfect timing.

Waiting is never easy. As I have mentioned before, I am not the most patient person. Once I know what I am supposed to do, I just want to go after it! It is easiest to hop on the path that gets you straight to the top and to your desired destination. But, when we do that, we shortcut God's plan and miss out on all the things He wants to teach us during our season of waiting.

I read a book a few years back called *The Jesus Hearted Woman* by Jodi Detrick. It was a great book that talked about essential leadership characteristics, especially for woman leaders. One of the ideas Jodi talked about was "Staircase Leadership." Jodi says in her book, "Some people are what I call 'elevator leaders'—they want a quick and easy ride to the top, skipping everything in between. But the strength to lead well when you get to the top, and the stamina to stay there, is built by taking the stairs…by putting one foot in front of the other, dealing with the incremental levels of leadership."

I love this comparison! While it is easiest to take the elevator to arrive right where we want to be in a short amount of time, we miss out on all the things we would have learned and all the experiences that would have shaped us if we took the stairs. We grow personally and in our relationship with the Lord when we take the road less traveled, or as Jodi likes to call it, "the stairs."

Even though I longed to go back on the missions field that summer, I was obedient and did not go. Yes, it killed me to look at all my friends' pictures who were going on summer missions because my heart was there! But, looking back on it all now, I know God had me right where He wanted me, and that summer was instrumental in preparing for Kingdom Kids Homes.

At 19, I was offered a part time job at my church in Tulsa, Oklahoma as the children's ministry director. I have always wanted to be on staff at a church, and this was definitely my dream job while I was in college! I started my new position during the summer of 2013. If I would have gone home or on missions, I would have missed out on the staff position God had for me at church. And let me tell you, being on staff at a church has taught me so much about ministry and about how to run an organization. During my last two years of college, I was able to oversee a section of ministry, which taught me a lot about overseeing my own ministry. I believe the dream of Kingdom Kids Homes would have definitely been delayed if I would not have gained the leadership experience I did from my church staff position. All in all, God knew I was supposed to stay put that summer, and I am glad He always knows what's best for His children.

That summer, I did go back to Michigan for two weeks to visit my family and friends. It was great to be back in my home church, Community Christian Church, while I was home. My church is very connected to Haiti, and I knew my Pastor, Tony Rea, had a huge heart for the nation of Haiti. God put on my heart to mention to him the vision of starting a home in Haiti. I was so nervous and did not even know how to bring up something like that to him. Starting an orphanage is not really something you bring up to your Pastor when you are having small talking with him for five minutes after church. But, I was only home for two weeks, so I knew I had limited time.

I was planning to do it the Sunday I was home. I did not know what I was going to say, but I knew I had to try. During service that day, my pastor happened to bring two missionaries on the stage who had their own missions organizations. They were talking about how the church financially supported their ministries. When I heard this, the devil began to discourage me. Thoughts came in my head like, *Look, the church already supports so many other mission organizations. They have too many. They could never support yours. Also, they already have established organizations; you have nothing but a dream. They are obviously going to support people like that over you.* With these thoughts rolling around in my head, I thought, *Yeah, there's no way I am mentioning my vision to him. God will provide for Kingdom Kids Homes in some way, just not through my church because they already have bigger and better things they are supporting.* I completely aborted my plan of mentioning the orphanage idea to my pastor.

After service, my mom and younger sister wanted to show me the new fellowship room they redid in the upstairs portion of our church. As we were walking to the elevator, my pastor came out of the church offices, and he offered to take us and show us the room. As we were headed there, he asked me if I was home for the whole summer. I told him that I was actually headed back to Tulsa to start as the director of the children's ministry at my church. He was surprised I was doing this and asked me if working at a church was what I wanted to do with my life. I said it was exactly what I would want to be doing while I was in college, but eventually I wanted to do full time missions ministry. About that time, my little sister, Melissa, blurted out "What she really wants to do is start an orphanage in Haiti!" The delivery was not the best, but the timing was pretty perfect. I was thankful Melissa had the courage to blurt out what I wanted to so badly.

After hearing this, my pastor looked at me in surprise. He said, "What? I did not know about this. You know, I have a lot of connections in Haiti. Do not try to do this by yourself. We want to help you and support you! Here's what I want you to do; go home, look at your schedule, and email me some times you can meet next week. I want you to come to my office and tell me all the dreams that God has put on your heart and everything you want to do in Haiti."

I walked away excited and in disbelief. I could not believe what had just happened! I wanted to have an opportunity to share my vision with him, but the devil had gotten inside my mind and tried to talk me out of it. But, as usual, God intervened and knew I had to share my dream with my pastor. I prayed that I would have the courage to ask my pastor to meet with him, but instead, he was the one asking to meet with me. Crazy how God works, huh?

That next week, I went into my pastor's office, and I shared with him the entire story and vision that God had given me. After hearing it, he encouraged me. He also told me about man he knew who owned land in a remote village in Northern

Haiti. This man already had a ministry that was working on the ground in Haiti. Pastor Tony informed me this man had a section of land he owned but was not using. He thought it would be a great place to put an orphanage and knew the orphan rate was high in that area. I was so excited to hear all of this and thought it sounded like a very promising lead. Finding and obtaining land in Haiti is very difficult, so to find an American man who already owned land would have been a huge advantage! My pastor told me he would contact the man who was in charge of this ministry, share my story with him, ask him about the land, and then we would meet again the next time I was home to discuss it further.

As I left my pastors office that day, I was very hopeful. It was scary for me to share the dream, especially with someone in a position of authority that could actually do something with it. I remember walking out of the church that day, with tears in my eyes, and saying out loud to myself, "Well, it's too late to turn back now."

Throughout the entire process of putting together Kingdom Kids Homes, I constantly said that to myself. Every time I shared the story with someone, every big step or small step forward I would take, I always found myself saying, "Looks like I have to do this, because it's too late to turn back now." Even when we made it as far as finding out the actual 16 kids that would be in our home, I still said "Too late to turn back now." Even though the time I walked out of my pastors office was the first official time I said and thought this out loud, the truth is the moment I said "Okay God, I'll do this for you, but you have to plop everything I need right into my lap" was the moment I should have been saying "It's too late to turn back now." Because the moment you say yes to God's plan, he's going to move, and he's going to use you no matter what. I heard one of my role models in the ministry, Dominic Russo, once say, "When you say yes and give God the tiniest bit of faith, together you will partner and change the world." There are not many more statements I have found to be more true. The moment you say yes to God's plan is the moment where it is too late to turn back.

And by the way, in case you were wondering, my home church, Community Christian Church, is a huge support to Kingdom Kids Homes today! Remember when the devil lied to me and told me they would never support me because they already supported so many other ministries? Well, looks like he was wrong! Don't ever let the devil discourage you or lie to you!

Personal Journal Entry

June 20th, 2013

I am already back in Tulsa! I came back here June 5th to start working at my church. I do miss home, but good things are definitely happening here, and I know I am right where God wants me to be, and there is truly no better feeling than that!

My time at home was really awesome, though! It was so great to spend time with my beautiful family, and every time I come home, I realize a little bit more that I have the greatest family in the world!

Also, something really awesome happened while I was home. I met with Pastor Tony and shared my Haiti dream with him. The way the whole meeting was set up was totally a God thing! One day after church, we were talking, and he heard I was going back to Tulsa to do children's ministry, and then, my little sister said something about me wanting to start an orphanage in Haiti! He said he wanted to meet with me and hear everything God had put on my heart and all my dreams (which is a lot). I met with him and shared everything about the Haiti vision. He was in total support and said he knows of a piece of land where I could possibly build the orphanage. He said that when I come home for Christmas we are going to meet and begin to talk about a plan! God is just working everything out. It is blowing my mind! Great things happen when we pray and trust in Him!

Chapter 8:
Haters Gonna Hate

I've told the story of Kingdom Kids hundreds of times, and when I share it, I usually share the highlights and the good times. Throughout the entire journey of the Kingdom Kids Homes dream coming to life, there have been so many "God moments." Moments that you sit back and think, Wow, how did that even happen? They are moments that are so miraculous there is no way any human could have orchestrated them. My story is filled with miraculous, God moments, and I love sharing those. I believe that when I get to share my God moments, it moves other people to start praying and seeking God for their own moments. But despite the many great moments, the journey to launching Kingdom Kids Homes was also filled with difficult ones.

When you pursue a God-given dream, the devil will put whatever obstacles he can in your path to slow you down and maybe even stop you. Sadly, those obstacles can be more than just poor circumstances; some of them can even be people.

After sharing the Kingdom Kids vision with my pastor in the spring of 2013, I was filled with excitement and energy. My spirits were pretty high after he told me about the man he knew who owned land in Haiti. Land in Haiti is extremely hard to obtain. Not only because it costs a pretty penny to buy land but also when buying land, people in Haiti can be deceptive. For example, you could look at a piece of land with the guy who owns it and buy it from him. Then, you find out later that man never really owned the land, but that it was actually owned by someone else and he tricked you into giving him money for the land when he never actually owned it. Then, to actually buy that land, you would have to spend thousands and thousands of dollars again to get it from the right owner. As you can see, purchasing Haitian land is a very complicated ordeal. So, a man who already had land in Haiti who we knew and could trust sounded like the perfect set up.

I came home for Christmas break in December 2013, and I had a meeting set up with Pastor Tony and the missions board at Community Christian Church to talk about the next steps with my vision for Haiti. The meeting went great, and Dave, the missions board director, told me he would try to get in contact with the man they knew who owned the land in Haiti to set up a meeting with him. Two hours after I left the missions board meeting, Dave called me and said the man who owned the land wanted to meet for lunch the next day! I was so excited and said I could be there no problem.

This was huge! I was so excited to take this step forward and share my vision with someone who had the capability to make it come to life! This meeting could be life changing, and it had the potential to really set my dream into motion! The next day, I walked into that meeting extremely confident and excited. I thought this man's land was the answer to many prayers. But, over the course of my young life, I have learned an important lesson: Things do not always go as planned. We can plan out how things are going to go, but ultimately, what God wants always overrides what we come up with on our own. The cool part about that is, His plans are always better than our own! I love that my God always knows what's best for me, even when I do not understand.

I met this man for lunch along with a few other church leaders. I am going to refer to this man as "Joe." As I previously mentioned, I was so excited to share my vision with Joe, a man who was so connected and established in Haiti. But, moments after I met him, that excitement slowly began to fade away. Our lunch started with only small talk, and from the way that conversation went I could tell Joe seemed to be a sarcastic, cynical, and pessimistic person, which was the complete opposite of what I expected. What was once excitement began to shift into intimidation. I began to think, "Maybe it's not a good idea to share my fragile dream with this guy."

About that time, one of the church leaders, who was at the lunch, said, "Okay Kristie, how about you begin to tell Joe about the dream that God has put on your heart." Truthfully, I was nervous and did not want to tell him anymore, but considering we met so he could hear my dream, I figured I had better go ahead and tell him. So I did.

I told him the whole story from start to finish. I included the moment I had the original vision, the time I had the vision again, the trip I had to Haiti in 2012, which really impacted me, and how God had grown and shaped the dream in my heart over the past year. Personally, I thought it was a pretty cool story, but Joe did not seem to be amused. I felt like he was barely listening to what I was sharing. He seemed bored. When I had finally wrapped up, Joe rolled his eyes. He looked extremely annoyed, and the first thing he said to me was, "Well, to do something like this you need funds!" In my head, I thought, What? I needed funds?! I had no idea you needed funds to build an orphanage? (I hope you are catching my sarcasm.) Then he went on this long tangent about how it will be so hard to raise the money and how I will never be able to do it. He also told me, "Or maybe you will raise the funds. Then you'll have the home for a year, but you will never raise the money to sustain it. You'll lose the house, and the kids will be back out on the streets and worse off than they were in the first place!"

Safe to say, Joe was not up for giving me his land to build on. He did not believe I could do it at all, and he conveyed that to me in a very brutally honest way.

Unfortunately, Joe did not stop there. He went on to say some pretty hurtful things. Joe said, "You know, you got to make sure this is what God has for your life, because I do not know if it is. You need to think long and hard about it. Do you think this was my dream to have a ministry in Haiti? No! This was my parents dream, and it was dropped into my lap!"

After Joe said that, I realized why he was so against me starting this ministry and building this house. Ministry in Haiti was not Joe's dream, but he felt obligated to take on the ministry his parents started and handed down to him, their son. Joe was stuck doing something he did not love and was not passionate about, something he dreaded doing. No wonder he was trying to get me to stop before I even started. In the midst of me really focusing on holding back tears, I also felt bad for Joe. He was the one not living what God had called him to do, but he was stuck living out someone else's purpose instead of walking in what God had for his life. It was not a healthy situation, and obviously, Joe had grown very bitter.

After Joe was almost through with his long, torturous, brutally honest lecture, one of the church leaders I was with tried to ask a question to smooth over the tension. He said, "So Joe, Kristie is headed back to college in about a week and is planning on taking some pretty serious steps towards pursing this dream, do you have any advice for her on where she should start?"

Joe just laughed and with an eye roll he said, "Wow, I don't know. . . . Good luck getting people to even take you seriously!" With that final remark, I was one completely heart broken young girl. Joe ended the meeting by telling me to go back to school and to get my "marketing buddies" to put a presentation together on what I planned on doing. He told me after he saw this plan, we could further discuss the land he owned in Haiti.

I was proud of myself because I did not shed a tear in front of Joe, but I did break down the moment I got to my car. My dream had just been shattered into pieces, and the guy who was my one promising lead just laughed at my dream and told me good luck getting people to take me seriously. I was so heart broken and confused.

I cried all the way home and basically kept crying for the remainder of the day. I knew pursing the dream God put on my heart would not be easy, but I had not expect it to be that difficult. Technically Joe did not say no. He wanted me to present a project to him. That door was technically still cracked open, but in my mind, it was shut. Even if Joe was willing to sell or give his land to me, he would always have a say in what Kingdom Kids Homes did. After hearing this guys heart and seeing his attitude towards ministry, I didn't even want to give this guy the tiniest foothold in the project. Honestly, I never wanted to lay eyes on or speak to the guy again . . . much less work with him! But, the land Joe owned was my only promising lead, and I did not really have any other options. I had hit a major obstacle on my journey to building Kingdom Kids Home. The strongest lead I had, actually the only lead I had, fell through. I was down, discouraged, and confused.

In the midst of the heartbreak, God saw me. Even though this was a very sad and hard part in the story, it was a critical turning point. I mentioned before how God always knows what is best, and as I reflect on this part in the story, I am brought to tears when I think about how God was right there with me even in that dark and confusing time.

During this season in my life, I remember clinging to Psalm 91. I felt the following verses were written exactly for me:

Whoever dwells in the shelter of the Most High will rest in the shadow of the Almighty. I will say of the Lord, "He is my refuge and my fortress, my God, in whom I trust." Surely he will save you from the fowler's snare and from the deadly pestilence. He will cover you with his feathers, and under his wings you will find refuge; his faithfulness will be your shield and rampart. You will not fear the terror of night, nor the arrow that flies by day, nor the pestilence that stalks in the darkness, nor the plague that destroys at midday. A thousand may fall at your side, ten thousand at your right hand, but it will not come near you.

Psalm 91:1-7 (NIV)

Even though the enemy was putting obstacles in my path and doing whatever he could to stop me, God had me and my dream right where He needed us to be—in the palm of His hand.

One of the most inspirational stories I have ever heard about a girl who overcame massive obstacles on the road to pursuing her dream is the story of Jennifer Bricker. Jennifer's dream was to be a world-class gymnast, which is hard enough to do with all of your body parts in tact and fully functioning. Unfortunately, not all Jennifer's body parts were in tact. She was born without legs.

Jennifer's real parents put her up for adoption when she was a baby. Fortunately, she was adopted by two loving parents who instilled in her a certain phrase from a very young age: "Never say can't." Even though Jennifer did not have legs, she dreamed of being a tumbler. Jennifer took her parents words to heart and learned to tumble, despite the massive obstacle of having no legs to tumble on. By the time Jennifer reached high school, she was crowned the tumbling champion of the state of Illinois!

Jennifer did not stop trying to reach her dream just because she was handicapped. She did not let all the obstacles standing in her way hold her back. Instead, she let them fuel her fire to dream bigger, practice more, and try harder.

Today, she is a famous acrobat and gymnast. She has toured with famous people, such as Britney Spears, and has performed in professional shows at New York's Lincoln Center. Jennifer pursed her dream of tumbling wholeheartedly, despite the limited ability she had. I am sure a lot of people thought Jennifer was crazy when she told them she would be a professional tumbler without any legs. Through all the doubts, Jennifer preserved, and with a lot of hard work, stamina, and determination, she reached her destination.

Yes, it is extremely tough to trust God when you are in a tough situation and you do not see a way out. But, let me encourage you to trust and put your faith in Him anyway, because not only does He always have a plan, but He has the best plan.

What Joe did not know was that I was not just a girl who woke up one day with a nice idea to help out some homeless children in a foreign country because it sounded like fun. He did not understand that this was God's purpose for my life. This was a God-ordained vision that He placed within the very depths of my heart. It was something I thought and prayed about everyday. It was something where when I thought of it, my eyes would instantly fill with tears and my heart would just burn with passion to help people I did not even know. Since the time I was knit together in my mother's womb, God knew that I would open Kingdom Kids Home on June 28th, 2015. This was my purpose. And once you've tasted purpose, it's hard to turn away and do anything else.

Personal Journal Entry from My Prayer Journal:

December 17, 2013

Dear Heavenly Father,

I thank You for Your favor in my life. I thank You for the right doors to be opened as I am taking steps and pressing into what I feel You have called me to do. I am going after what I know You have created me to do and what I am made for. I pray for favor, wisdom, clarity, answers, and open doors as I go into my meeting with Pastor Tony and the missions board tomorrow. I pray I can effectively communicate my heart, my vision, and the dream You have laid on my heart for my ministry and for this Haiti project. It has been a long road, and I am thankful for all the doors You have opened so far. Let this be a significant meeting where we take major steps into making this orphanage and this dream a reality. I thank You for this vision, God. I pray that you remain the center of it all. Guide my every step. I need You. Expand and enlarge my faith through this. God, I don't think I've ever wanted anything more than to see this orphanage built, the beautiful children rescued, lives healed, and restored, and many souls welcomed into Your kingdom! I thank You for calling me for such a time as this. I thank You for placing every vision in my heart. This plan was handcrafted for me in the heart and mind of God before I was even born! I was made to do this. You have heard my every cry and every prayer I have sent up over this dream. Therefore…

I will be blessed because my confidence is in YOU and my trust is in YOU. I will be like a tree planted by the water. I will not fear when the heat comes or a tough situation arises; my leaves will always be green and I will not be taken down because the joy of the Lord is my strength! I will have no worries in the year of drought or about how the finances will work out. I will never fail to bear fruit and lead people closer to God no matter what season I am in.

The Kristie version of Jeremiah 17:7–8

I thank You, God, that You know and see my heart, and You will answer my every prayer. All my hope is in You and my heart is Yours.

Amen.

Chapter 9:
Joy Comes in the Morning

I woke up the next morning feeling a little bit better. I thought to myself, Joe is just one guy with one opinion. He did not know me or my heart at all, and he obviously did not know how big my God was. My God parted the Red Sea so the Israelites could walk through when the Egyptians were right on their heels. My God shut the mouths of the lions when Daniel was thrown into a den full of them. My God impregnated a young, normal, virgin girl to bring our Savior into the World. Making the way and opening the doors for me to start this home would be a small task for Him.

That morning, my mom walked into my room. She said to me, "Kristie, I was watching Joel Olsteen on TV this morning, and what he was saying was exactly for you! He was talking about never letting people deny the dream that God has placed on your heart. When he had the dream to start a church, he met with people and shared his dream, and they said he was not a good enough speaker and he would never pastor a church—and now he has one of the biggest churches in America! He also said when Shaquille O'neal tried out for his high school basketball team, he got cut. The coach told him he was too big and awkward when he ran up and down the court, and now he is one of the biggest basketball players in the NBA! You need to continue to pursue the dream that God has put on your heart and not let what people say knock you down."

Thank God for Godly and supportive parents, huh? But, what my mom was saying was exactly right. I said, "You're right mom! I was thinking this morning about people in the Bible who had a God given dream, and every single one of them had a big obstacle or someone in their way who tried to stop them, but they trusted in God anyways. That's what I am going to do! I have no idea how this is going to work out, but I know I have to keep going after it because it is what God has called me to do. I would rather know that I did everything I could to obey God and end up failing, than live knowing I quit the moment I hit a road bump. I do not know how it is going to be done, but I am going to build this home and prove Joe wrong!"

There are so many stories in the Bible and throughout history where people had a huge call of God on their lives and many difficulties in their path to reaching what God had called them to do. One great woman in history who was called by God, but hit a lot of road bumps along her journey, was Joan of Arc. I do not know if you know a lot about her life because I did not until I recently read a book about her. After reading about Joan's life, I was so inspired. Angels spoke to Joan and specifically told her that she was supposed to rescue France from the English and take the rightful French leader to the city of Reims to be crowned as the King of France. This was no small task, and did I mention Joan was only 16 when she was called to do this! Talk about overwhelming. Joan did not know the first thing about leading an army, but she knew what she heard was from God, and she needed to take her call seriously. She was a courageous young girl and set up a meeting to share what she had been called to do with the Governor. He listened to her and then discouraged her call, said she was crazy, and sent her home. (Sounds kind of familiar right?)

Even though Joan's call from the Lord had been completely shot down by a powerful person, she kept her faith and did not give up because she knew this was what God had created her to do. This was her calling! Joan, who was now 17, got to see the Governor a second time, and he sent her away again saying that her ideas were preposterous. After being rejected a second time, history records Joan saying, "I must be at the King's side. There will be no help if not from me. Although I would have rather remained spinning at my mother's side . . . yet I must go and do this thing, for my Lord wills that I do so." I love this quote from Joan because it shows that she was not choosing the comfortable or easy path. It would have been easy for her to just stay at home, living a comfortable life with her family by her side. But that's the thing about a call from God, you are not okay with just doing what is comfortable.

You are called by God when you cannot rest or settle for normal, when you know what God is calling you to is out there, waiting for you to do it, still unaccomplished.

The third time Joan of Arc went to the Governor, the presence of God was truly with her, and the Holy Spirit revealed to her something about the Governor that no one knew. When she told him, he was finally convinced that God was speaking to this young girl and agreed to listen to her and to help her save France. Years later, that is exactly what Joan of Arc did. She led the French army to victory over the English and took the rightful ruler of France to Reims to be crowned King of France, just as God told her she would do.

Do you want to know Joan of Arc's secret to success? She did not give up, and she kept her faith. She kept God at the center of her vision every step of the way. History records that when tough times came during the war and out on the battlefield, Joan would go away for a time of prayer, while others rested. She knew that in order to fulfill her call she had to keep Christ at the center, and she had to let Him guide her every step of the way.

I knew in that moment, when I was down and discouraged because some man I hardly knew squashed my dream, that was what I had to do too. I had to keep my faith, and I had to not give up.

When I think of someone who kept her faith through a discouraging time, I think of the woman in the Bible who had the issue of blood. This story takes place in Mark 5:25. This woman had been sick with a blood disease for 12 years!

She spent all the money she had on doctors, trying to get well. This did not help her condition at all. In fact, her condition only continued to get worse. One day, when Jesus was going through this woman's town, she knew she had to get through to Him. This woman says in Mark 5:28, "If I even touch his garments, I will be made well" (ESV). Wow, talk about keeping the faith! This woman trusted God so much for her healing, that she believed she only had to touch Him. After nothing had worked for the past 12 years, she had faith that Jesus was her healer. And we know how it ends. The Bible says in Mark 5:29 that when she touched Him immediately the flow of blood dried up, and the disease left her body. Jesus said to this woman, "Daughter, your faith has made you well; go in peace, and be healed of your disease" (Mark 5: 34, ESV).

This woman had such deep faith to believe that God could heal her after nothing else had worked. After having this disease for 12 years, I think it's safe for us to assume this woman was pretty frustrated and discouraged. But despite what the doctors and doubters were saying, she kept her faith. She did not give up, and she trusted in God, in the midst of a very difficult time.

Even though the meeting with Joe broke my heart and left me feeling discouraged and confused, I was glad it happened. Yes, I was down for the night, but my joy came back in the morning! That meeting made me more determined than ever to see the vision through because, like Joan, I knew in my heart that it was what God had created me to do, and I was not going to let a little discouragement allow me to abandon God's call. In spite of the obstacles and confusion I was facing, I was going to choose to keep my faith and trust God anyway. And when I chose to cling to my Savior and trust Him in the midst of the heartbreak and confusion, that is when things started to turn around.

Personal Journal Entry:

January 17, 2014

As for the Haiti plan, I have made a lot of progress this past Christmas break. Praise the Lord! First, I met with Pastor Tony and Dave (the church mission board director) and talked about using the land in Bocazelle, Haiti for the orphanage. They set up a meeting for me to meet with Joe, the guy who owns the land we want to build on in Haiti. This man was beyond rude, and he totally shot down my dream. He pretty much told me it would impossible to find the support and raise the money to build the orphanage. He also told me I would have a hard time finding people who would actually take me seriously. This broke my heart, and I was holding back tears the entire meeting! At the end, after he basically smashed all my hopes and dreams, he didn't say no. He told me to go back to ORU, put together a plan and presentation of what I wanted to do, and then meet with him when I am home for spring break to give him my best "sales pitch." After all that, we could start a conversation about the land in Haiti. Once I hit my car, I let it out and cried all the way home. I felt like I had just got my heart broken. I was so confused and unsure if I wanted to even use him as a connection to get land in Haiti because, honestly, I really don't care to see that man again!

My family really came through for me in that moment. They were all supportive, especially my mom. And when the orphanage does get built, a lot of credit will go to her because I don't think I would have been able to carry out the dream without her encouragement. She mentioned to me all these great people who rose up and followed their dream, despite the people who doubted them. Then, I got to thinking: all the world changers I know of have been told no or that they cannot do it by someone. Joe was just the first of mine! I decided I am not going to quit. I am going to keep going and come up with a plan that will knock Joe off his feet.

Chapter 10:
In His Hands

After making the conscious decision not give up on my dream, doors started to open and things started to take off. The week after my meeting with Joe, I had a meeting set up with some friends named, Daniel and Lizzy, who run an evangelistic missions ministry out of Michigan. Their ministry takes teams of young people on missions trips where they put on evangelistic crusades in third world nations. I wanted to share with them the vision that God had given to me to start an home in Haiti, and I wanted to receive some feedback and advice on launching a ministry. I also updated Daniel and Lizzy on my meeting with Joe. This meeting could not have been more different than my meeting with him. These two were so encouraging and supportive. They helped restore my confidence!

After I finished sharing my heart with the two of them, Daniel told me that his ministry was taking a team to Haiti that summer, and he invited me to come along. He told me that I could come down with the team, but during the day I could meet up with the people and connections I had lined up. He also promised to introduce me to his contacts and leaders who worked on the ground to set things up in Haiti. He said they would be the people to know if I wanted to launch any kind of ministry on the ground in Haiti. This sounded amazing, and I was so grateful for the opportunity! I was excited to explore the connections that were out there, and I was definitely excited to get back on the missions field.

It had been too long!

After the meeting with Daniel and Lizzy, I had a few more days in Michigan before I had to head back to Oklahoma to finish the second half of my junior year. My meeting with them was on a Thursday, and I was scheduled to fly out on Saturday afternoon. As I was packing up my things Saturday morning, my mom came into my room and informed me that my flight was cancelled due to bad weather, and they had rescheduled me to fly out on Sunday morning instead. So I stopped packing and started to hang out with my sister. About an hour and a half later, my mom came back and said that my flight was actually back on again. By this point, my flight was taking off in an hour and there was no way I could pack, make it to the airport, and board the flight in that short amount of time. We kept my newly scheduled Sunday morning departure and found it really odd that my flight was cancelled for less than two hours and was now back to normal again. My sister Shelby said, "Well, maybe this happened for a reason." I laughed and thought, What is the plane going to crash or something? I was excited my flight was moved because that meant I was able to attend the missions party happening at my church that night. Daniel and Lizzy were hosting a get together at our church for anyone who had been on a past trip with their ministry or anyone who was going on a future trip with them. I was excited to meet people who would be on the same trip to Haiti that coming summer.

I went to the party that night and had a great time. After hearing about what our team would be doing in Haiti, I was really excited to go! As the meeting was finishing up, Lizzy came up and told Daniel she had one more thing she felt like she had to share. She grabbed the mic, and before I knew it, I was being called out. Lizzy shared how she and Daniel had met with me a few days earlier and how she felt like everyone should lay hands on me and pray for this big dream God had put on my heart. I was shocked and a little embarrassed because I had hardly told anyone about this huge, secret dream I had, and now a whole room of people knew. It was another one of those, "Too late to turn back now" moments.

Everyone came around me and prayed for me. It was such a powerful moment, and the presence of God was very evident. I was thankful for the prayer and thought to myself, *This moment was definitely worth having my flight changed.* I felt so encouraged after being lifted up in prayer that night. But, little did I know, something else was about to happen.

After the meeting had officially ended and everyone was hanging out and chatting, a guy I had never met before came up to me and started asking me a lot of questions about the home and ministry I was planning on launching. I was answering his questions when he asked how I planned on raising the funds I needed for the home. I told him that I honestly had not thought too much about that part since I was mainly focused on laying the groundwork to start the home. He told me once I got things more established he would love to contribute financially and be a monthly supporter of Kingdom Kids Homes. I was so excited! About 15 minutes later, right before I was about to leave, he came up to me, said a final word of encouragement, handed me fifty dollars, and said, "Here, let this be a start." And just like that I received my first monetary donation for Kingdom Kids Homes.

It is crazy how God works. I missed my flight, went to an event, met a stranger, and picked up my first financial supporter for Kingdom Kids Homes without even trying. In that moment, I wanted to call Joe, who a week before told me I would never raise the money for this project, and say, "Hey, a guy I just met handed me our first donation, and I did not even have to ask!"

After this, I was so encouraged and was fully confident that God saw me, knew my needs, and would open all the doors I needed along this journey, doors that would even blow my mind. Doors so amazing, I would have to write a book just to tell of all the awesome miracles God performed on the road to reaching my destination.

One thing I learned from this part in my story is that sometimes we do not know what God is up to. We do not know why we have to meet people who discourage us, we do not know why we have to face heartbreak, and we do not know why things get mixed up and why flights get changed. But the best part is, God knows. Through it all, he has everything under control. I love the verses of Isaiah 41:8-13, that says:

> But you, Israel, my servant, Jacob, ***whom I have chosen***, you descendants of Abraham my friend, I took you from the ends of the earth, from its farthest corners ***I have called you***. I said, 'You are my servant'; ***I have chosen you*** and have not rejected you. So ***do not fear, for I am with you***. Do not be dismayed for I am your God. I will ***strengthen you and help you; I will uphold you*** with my righteous hand. All who rage against you will surely be ashamed and disgraced; those who oppose you will be as nothing and perish. Though you search for your enemies, ***you will not find them***. Those who rage against you will be ***as nothing at all***. For I am the Lord your God who takes hold of your right hand and says to you, ***Do not fear; I will help you.***
>
> Isaiah 41:8-13 (NIV)

Every time I read that passage, I am filled with so much peace and comfort. Those verses are proof that when God calls us to do something big for His kingdom, we do not have to be afraid, and we do not have to worry about how it is all going to pan out, because He's got us. God will defeat anything that tries to come against us because we are His!

It will not always be easy when believers are following after God and striving to live a life pleasing to Him. There will be confusing times. I am sure Daniel was confused as to why he was being thrown into a den full of hungry lions when he was trying to grow in his relationship with the Lord by praying three times a day. Daniel is the definition of a leader. He stood his ground and did what was right, even when it was against the law to do so. In Daniel's day, there was a decree saying no man should pray to any other god or person for thirty days other than King Darius. Despite the law, Daniel did not stop praying and seeking the Lord. When the officials heard this, they became angry and urged the king to throw Daniel into the lions den. Even in the face of death, Daniel trusted God and believed God was holding his life in His hands. That is exactly what God was doing. He shut the lions' mouths, and Daniel came out of the lions' den—alive, unharmed, and without a scratch. Even in the midst of a scary and unsure situation, Daniel pressed into God. He still prayed and believed in God when everyone was against him. He knew God was holding him, even when he could not see the end result.

When God gives us a dream or a big vision, this is what we must do too. Despite the obstacles, people who will tear you down, and confusing times, we must choose to trust that God sees us and that He is holding us in His hands.

After that night, I was fully convinced that God saw me and He was working on my behalf. With a huge dream and a little bit of money (50 dollars to be exact) in my pocket, I was ready to fully pursue my call and to confidently go after the huge vision God had put on my heart. I did not know how it was all going to end up, but I would continue to move forward, trusting that I was in God's hands . . .which is the best place to be.

Personal Journal Entry from My Prayer Journal:

February 18, 2014

Dear Heavenly Father,

Wow, I love reading over my past prayers because they are proof of how faithful You are and how You have truly been holding me in Your hands. You have been leading me every step of the way. Let me never forget Your faithfulness and how You have walked with me all through my life. Great are you, Lord! There is truly no one like You in all the earth! I am nothing without you, and if You were not with me, I would be nowhere.

    Lord, I thank You for the way things are coming together with the orphanage and how You are piecing every detail together little by little. I thank You for knowing every thought and concern that is on my mind and for taking care of each one! Help me to remember all this is for Your glory. Let me not take any credit for this. I am just thankful and humbled You would use me to do this work in Your kingdom. Let me keep a humble and thankful attitude no matter what. Let me turn every second of praise I may receive and give it right back to You . . . because this is completely Yours, and I would not have the slightest clue what I was doing if it weren't for You. Your love, Lord, is incomparable and better than words.

I thank You for the joy You are constantly bringing me. Through the entire process of starting Kingdom Kids Homes—through the exciting and prosperous times and the freak out moments—let me keep Your joy rooted deep down in my heart. Let it be rooted so deep that no person or circumstance can take it away. No matter what obstacles I face, let Your joy override the problems and let it withstand, even in the toughest of times. I thank You for making me strong in the areas where I am weak.

It's crazy what can happen when believers just say "yes" to your plan! Man, I never imagined I would be where I am at, so quickly, and at this young of an age. But, I thank You for making BIG things happen when we step out on a limb and trust in You.

Continue to blow my mind, Lord. Open up doors, and provide in huge ways where I sit back and think, How did this even happen?

I am trusting You with this whole situation, Lord. You have it in Your hands, and I know You will not let me fall. Give me Your boldness and confidence when I meet with people and share the vision with them. Let Your heart speak through me. Continue to open doors for financial provision, and let the funds come pouring in.

I cannot wait for the day I cut the ribbon and we dedicate the first Kingdom Kids Home to You! I know it will be one of the best moments of my life. I cannot wait to get on my knees in the middle of the orphanage and say: "Lord, this home is a testimony and evidence of your faithfulness. It is living proof of how You can use a normal 18-year-old girl with a God-given dream to do something beautiful for your kingdom."

My God, I thank You there is nothing too big for You, and with You, all things are possible. Love you more than life itself.

Amen.

Chapter 11:
Open Doors

The next day, I headed back to ORU to start the second semester of my junior year of college. I slowly began to tell a few people and close friends about the vision God had placed on my heart to start an orphanage in Haiti, but I was very selective with whom I told. The main reason I started cluing some close friends in to what was going on was so they could join me in praying for big doors to open. When you have a God-given dream, you need to be careful whom you share it with. I also wanted to be a woman of my word and did not want to tell a lot of people I was going to do this big thing and then not have it happen. A lot of people are really great at talking about doing something, but when it comes to actually accomplishing the task, they never deliver. I did not want to be one of those people. Since some big, important doors were starting to open, I thought I would share my dream with a few friends whom I trusted and whom I would ask to pray with me. To this day, I am still so grateful for all the friends who prayed for me and encouraged me along the way! I do not know if Kingdom Kids Homes would have happened without all of them! But, let me encourage you; if God has put a huge dream on your heart, be very selective with whom you share it with. Unfortunately, some people will use it as an opportunity to discourage you and to tear you down. Prayerfully consider whom you should share your dream with. Share it with people you trust and those who will speak words of life over the call God has placed on you.

Also, do not go bragging about this incredible task God has called you to do. Choose to be like Mary, a girl who had a huge call from God, but chose to treasure the things God spoke to her in her heart. Everyone has a call from God on their lives, but there is no doubt Mary had the most unique call of all. To this day, no one else can say God called them to bring the Savior of the universe, Jesus Christ, into the world. When an angel of the Lord appeared to Mary and informed her she would bring the Savior into existence, she did not say, "Well I am a pretty amazing person, so no wonder God would choose me." She did not go shouting from the rooftops that God had chosen her to be the mother of the Savior of the world. Instead, she was surprised and asked, "How can this be?" The angel told Mary she was highly favored in the eyes of the Lord. Was Mary's family well known and wealthy? Did Mary have a degree from an Ivy League school? No. In fact, she was only a teenage girl when she received word of her call from the angel. She was an ordinary girl who was devoted to serving God. The Lord saw Mary, a young girl who had a humble and willing heart, and chose to use her to play a part in changing the world. God seems to have a habit of using ordinary people whose hearts are devoted to Him. When you put God first, have a humble attitude and a willing and obedient heart, you will also be "highly favored" in the eyes of the Lord. Those are the kinds of people God is looking to use.

Once I was back in Tulsa, I shared with my pastor the vision God had given me a few years before. He was very supportive and suggested I meet with his friend who had recently started a girls home in Ghana. I met with his friend, Steve, and two of the interns who served in their ministry for lunch one afternoon. I asked Steve a lot of questions about what it takes to start a home in a foreign country. He was so helpful and gave me a lot of guidance. He also said he would show me examples of their business plans and the legal work they had to set up to start their home. All of the information Steve offered me was extremely helpful. One of the interns was around my age, and we really hit it off. She told me that her uncle, Matt, currently lived in Haiti. He moved there to start a business, and she suggested that I get in contact with him and share with him what I was wanting to do in Haiti.

Matt and I began to exchange emails. One night in February 2014, I got an email from him that broke my heart. We were talking about meeting up when I visited Haiti that summer, and in his email he described to me a desolated and corrupt children's home in Haiti he wanted me to visit with him on my trip.

His email said this:

"I recently found a group of 13 children living in an "orphanage" whose conditions were complete squalor. They are barely surviving. I would love to see someone do something to help these children. The Haitian who started this "orphanage" is not necessarily the type of person you think he is. People like this see an orphanage as a business and hope by collecting these poor children, that wealthy donors will donate money that he can use to elevate his life as well. It is a well-known way to escape poverty by starting an organization or orphanage."

When I read Matt's email describing the living conditions and the horrible situation these Haitian children were in, I immediately began to cry. My heart was breaking for these children whom I had never seen or met. For the rest of the week I could not get the news of those kids out of my mind, and I was more fired up than ever to start a children's home in Haiti to rescue helpless children who were stuck in the same type of situation. I replied to Matt and told him that home would be on the top of my list of places to visit while I was in Haiti that summer.

During this time, I also was having conversations with a man who owned a building company in the US, but did charity work building houses in Haiti. You might be wondering how I found this guy? Google, actually! About a month before I contacted the owner of this building company, Mike, I was randomly Google searching "Building an orphanage in

Haiti" to try to clue myself in a little on what it would take to build a home like this in a third-world nation. One of the results that came up was Mike's charity. I clicked on it and read that this was a charity that built homes for people in Haiti, and the crazy part is, it was based out of a city in Michigan about 30 minutes from where I grew up! I thought, This is crazy! They could be located anywhere in the world, but they are so close to me. As I was reading about the work Mike and his team did in Haiti, I felt the Holy Spirit speak to me saying, "You need to contact this guy." I thought, Yeah, no way. Me, a random stranger, calling up this business owner saying, "Hey, God is calling me to start a home in Haiti…how do I go about building that?" Does not sound crazy at all, right? I thought, That would be so weird… I am not doing that!

I decided to shoot this guy an email, despite how crazy doing so sounded. I figured that the worst thing that could have happened would be to not get a response back or have him say "Sorry kid, not interested," so I figured I did not have much to lose. I sent Mike a brief email sharing with him what I wanted to do, and I asked if I could have a phone conversation with him to ask him some questions. I got an email response the next day from him saying this:

Kristie,

Great to hear from you. Let's try to connect this week. I look forward to hearing more.

Best,
Mike

I was ecstatic to receive this response! The next week, Mike and I talked on the phone. I asked him many questions, and he was very supportive and encouraging. An hour and a half and four pages of notes later, we finished our phone call, and I actually felt like I had a pretty good idea of what it would look like to build something in Haiti. Mike also gave me the name and contact information for his contractor and the architect he used when building his projects in Haiti. He talked to me a lot about how hard it is to find someone you can trust to oversee building projects, but these two men were trustworthy and would do the job right. I was so grateful for Mike's guidance. Soon after our phone call, I contacted his architect and contractor and set up meetings with both of them on my upcoming summer trip.

Things were coming together! By the end of the second semester of my junior year, I had a entire weeks worth of meetings lined up for my Haiti trip in the end of June. As I write this and reflect on that season of my life, I am still amazed by all the doors God opened and all the crazy connections I made that put me exactly on the path I needed to be on to open Kingdom Kids Home.

One of my favorite quotes is from Mark Batterson's book, *The Circle Maker*. He says, "Work as if it depends on you, and pray as if it depends on God." As I reflect on my life and the road to opening Kingdom Kids Home, there is nothing I know to be truer! When God gives you a vision, it will require work on your part to see it through. Sometimes it will involve contacting people you've never met to ask for help or feeling a little crazy when you share your dream with someone you haven't even laid eyes on before. It may involve you pushing and fighting for the vision even when you have no clue how it is all going to come together. You will have to choose to take risks and to follow the voice of the Holy Spirit, even when it may seem crazy. If you want to see your God-given dream come to pass, you will have to work hard. You will have to be relentless until the dream comes to life. But at the end of the day, your hard work alone will never be enough. You can push for your dream and maneuver situations to have the odds be in your favor, but without God's divine power and favor, your God given vision will not come to pass. Yes, you need to work hard, but you also need to pray, trust God, and obey what he is leading you to do, even when it may not make sense. And believe me, when you combine hard work with faith in God, there is no way you will fail. In fact, God will work things together behind the scenes and fit all of the details together so perfectly it will blow your mind. If He did it for me, I know He will do it for you!

Personal Journal Entry:

December 26, 2014

Right now, I feel like I can relate to Mary when she prays this in Luke 1:46-52: "My soul glorifies the Lord and my spirit rejoices in my God my Savior, for he has been mindful if the <u>humble state</u> of his servant…he has performed mighty deeds with his arms; he has scattered those who are proud in his in most thoughts. He has brought down rulers from their thrones, but he has <u>lifted up the humble</u>."

 I am still amazed that God would use me, such a normal girl with an ordinary upbringing, to do huge things for His kingdom. I can relate to Mary when she says, "For he has been mindful of the humble state of his servant" and I am thankful God chooses to use ordinary, normal people to do extraordinary things for His kingdom. I will forever be amazed by how God continues to prove himself faithful in my life. If God is for me, who or what could be against me?

Chapter 12:
Bold Prayers

The time had finally arrived! It was the middle of June in 2014, and I was just one week away from going on my trip to Haiti. This trip was going to be huge. During my time in Haiti, I would be meeting with people who had ministries there, orphanage directors, pastors, contractors, and different Haitian contacts to begin to figure out the game plan for starting Kingdom Kids Home in Haiti that next summer. After all, God did tell me I would figure out the plan during summer 2014 and I would open the home in summer 2015, after I graduated from college. I was not completely confident in that time frame, but I told the Lord I would shoot for it! I could not believe the time had already come to go on the "planning trip."

You are probably reading this thinking, "Wow, that is a lot of pressure!" You bet it was! I remember being so nervous that week, and it seemed like every moment I wasn't talking to someone, I was praying. During my personal quiet time, I was reading about Nehemiah. I love Nehemiah's bold, wise, and courageous leadership. Nehemiah moved forward with the vision God put on his heart, even when people doubted him and even when some wanted to take his life. He was so sure and confident in following after what God was calling him to do. With a humble boldness, Nehemiah actively pursued his calling, and I remember praying for God to give me the same boldness He gave Nehemiah. I prayed He would make me humble. I did not want to show up in the country acting like I was the one who was going to save them all from their lifestyle of despair! But, I also prayed He would make me bold. Bold enough to continue to pursue what He was calling me to do when obstacles got in the way and when things were not looking so good.

About two days before the trip, I was sitting in my dorm room at ORU, and I read Joshua 1. When I read this chapter, I felt as if verses 1-9 were written just for me. It said:

> I will give you every place where you set your foot, as I promised Moses. Your territory will extend from the desert to Lebanon, and from the great river, the Euphrates—all the Hittite country—to the Mediterranean Sea in the west. No one will be able to stand against you all the days of your life. As I was with Moses, so I will be with you; I will never leave you nor forsake you. Be strong and courageous, because you will lead these people to inherit the land I swore to their ancestors to give them. Be strong and very courageous. Be careful to obey all the law my servant Moses gave you; do not turn from it to the right or to the left, that you may be successful wherever you go. Keep this Book of the Law always on

your lips; meditate on it day and night, so that you may be careful to do everything written in it. Then you will be prosperous and successful. Have I not commanded you? Be strong and courageous. Do not be afraid; do not be discouraged, for the Lord your God will be with you wherever you go.

Joshua 1:3-9, NIV

Speaking of Joshua, he was a man in the Bible who had a bold, big call from God. He was called to take over leading the children of Israel into the Promised Land after Moses died. We all know Moses was a strong, bold, and respectable leader among the Israelites. Stepping into a role of leadership where you are Moses' successor is a pretty big deal. It is clear Joshua felt inadequate to lead when in the first chapter of Joshua, God had to reassure him that he was called to do it, and that God was taking care of him and with him.

As we look at Joshua's journey while he is leading the Israelites, it is obvious that God is with him and that Joshua followed the voice of the Lord. Only the Lord would direct Joshua to lead the people to walk around the walls of Jericho for seven days in order to take the city captive. Despite his feelings of inadequacy or his feelings of intimidation, Joshua obeyed God, embraced his call, and led with excellence.

If you feel God calling you to do something but feel completely inadequate and over your head, I know how you feel. When God gives you a big call, you will feel unqualified, and the truth is, you are unqualified to do it alone. We need to invite God to direct and lead us every step of the way because with Him we are more than qualified. With Him, we are more than conquers. No problem, obstacle, vision, or dream is too big or too intimidating for God.

Going into the week-long Haiti trip, I felt a lot like Joshua did in chapter 1. But, I also felt God say to me the same things He said to Joshua in that chapter —- to be strong and courageous, to obey, to not fear, and that He was with me.

Right after I read the passage in Joshua 1, God started to speak to my heart. I quickly grabbed my journal and wrote down what He was saying. He told me:

June 8th, 2014

"Kristie, Joshua 1 is your chapter. Just as I used Joshua to change a nation despite the obstacles he faced, I will use you. I have called you and equipped you. I am with you, so whom should you fear? I am giving you every place you put your foot. Just trust in me. No one and nothing will be able to come against you or stop you because I am with you. This entire vision is Mine. I have called you to lead these children into My kingdom and lead people in this nation back to My heart. Stay close and locked in on Me and My promises, not what the people or circumstances around you are saying. Trust Me and obey Me throughout this entire process and you will come out victorious. Just as Moses and Joshua faced obstacles, so will you. That is why it is so important you stay pressed in and focused on me, just as they did. I am your anchor, and I am your hope when situations are looking dim. When you feel discouraged,

pour your heart out to Me and sit at my feet. Watch Me renew your strength. I am with you, Kristie. I will open the doors, and I will make a way, just as I did for Joshua. Just keep your eyes on Me."

My faith grew tremendously, and my fears began to shrink once God spoke to me. After hearing and writing down what God spoke to me, I began to pray. I remember this prayer as if it were yesterday. I sat back on my bed, and I said, "God, Haiti is next week, and I'm not going to lie. I am nervous. There are so many unknowns, and there is so much to figure out and plan in a week's time. But, I thank You for making the way and for making it an easy way. And Lord, I know this is a bold prayer, but I thank you that you are giving me every place I set my foot, and that you will just give us the land. I pray it will just plop it into our lap as you have done with so many other things. I pray the land You have set aside for us to build this house on will just be handed to us. I know that is a bold and nearly impossible prayer, but I believe and trust it is possible with You."

At times, it may feel like we are asking too much of God when we have a large prayer request. We think the huge request we have will burden or inconvenience God. We think of God in our human mindset and forget He is unlike any human. He is the creator of the universe, and anything is possible with Him. Bold prayers do not inconvenience or intimidate God. In fact, He wants His people to pray bold prayers and dream big dreams. He delights in that.

The next couple of days went by, and before I knew it, I was boarding my flight to Haiti. I was excited, nervous, and anxious to see what the Lord had in store for the upcoming week. I remember sitting on my flight to Port Au Prince, and I read a note that I had written in my phone a while back. The note said:

"If you do not have confidence and believe in your dream, then no one else will."

I do not remember who had said that or where I had heard it from, but it was exactly what I needed to hear as I was heading into a big week in Haiti to pursue my dream, full of unknowns. I remember sitting on the plane praying for God to give me the confidence I needed for the week ahead. I did not know what I would face, but I knew that my God was for me, so who could be against me?

Personal Journal Entry from My Missions Journal:

June 16, 2014

Dear Journal,

Well, I am back at it again! I am on a flight to Ft. Lauderdale right now, and in the morning, I will be back in Port Au Prince, Haiti! When I think of all God has done with the vision He placed on my heart over two years ago, I am in absolute awe. When God first gave me the vision for Kingdom Kids Home back in January 2012, my freshman year of college, I thought there is no way God could work through me to do something like that, especially not while I was in college! But, I prayed and said, "Fine God, if you want me to do this, you have to open all the doors and plop everything right into my lap, and I'll do it!" Looking back over the past two and a half years, I am blown away by how God has done just that! During the next week in Haiti, I will be meeting with many different contacts, orphanage directors, pastors, a contractor, an architect, and I will be looking at potential locations to put the orphanage. I cannot believe this week I will begin to pursue the calling God has placed on my life since I was six years old! The more I get into this stuff, the more I realize there is nothing I would rather do for the rest of my life! I am so grateful for all the ways God has been providing left and right! I am expecting big things to happen this week! There are so many unknowns, which can be a little nerve wracking. But, I know God's hand is all over *this project, and He would not bring me this far and provide for me all He has provided just to let me fail.*

Joshua 1:1-9 is my focus for this week and for this entire project. I feel as if God is saying this to me, just like He said these things to Joshua many years ago:

> *"Every place the sole of your foot will tread upon I have given to you. There will not be any man that will be able to stand against you. Just as I was with Moses, I will be with you. I will not fail you, and I will not forsake you. Be strong and of good courage. Follow the Word of God, and you will be prosperous wherever you go. Do not let My word depart from You, but meditate on it day and night. Then, I will make you prosperous and you will find great success. I command you to be strong and of good courage; do not be afraid and do not be dismayed, for the Lord your God is with you wherever you go."*

I know God is with me and for me. I know He has called me for such a time as this. With God on my side, there's no way I can lose.

Chapter 13:
A Divine Meeting

We hit the ground running the minute we landed in Haiti. Once we got to our hotel, we put our luggage in our rooms, and a half hour later, Matt (my friend's uncle who wanted to show me the desolated orphanage) picked us up. We were pretty tired since we had slept in the airport the night before, but we did not let that slow us down. We had a job to do, and only a week to accomplish everything!

My dad, my friend Miranda, and I loaded into Matt's SUV and headed to the house of an American missionary living with his family in Haiti. His name was Tommy, and he was the one who discovered this horrible situation along with his translator, Robinson. Tommy and Robinson were taking us to the desolated "orphanage." Once we were at Tommy's house, he gave us more details on the destructive man running this home while we were waiting for Robinson to arrive. Tommy said this man would take these children away from their families, promising the parents who could not afford to take care of their children that he would give them a better life. But in reality he barely took care of the children at all. These children hardly ate, did not have much clothing, and were in poor medical condition. Also, the so-called "house" they lived in was two slabs of concrete partially covered by a small roof. This man would take Americans back to this place and tell them he could not afford to take care of these children and needed money to keep his children alive. After seeing a sight as horrendous as that little shack, most Americans would hand him money without thinking twice about it. This man would keep the money for himself and not give any to the children. He was using the kids as a way to become rich and take care of himself—he did not care about the wellbeing of the children at all. He was a Haitian con artist.

Sadly, situations like this one are pretty common in Haiti. Because I never felt called to live in Haiti, the more I heard stories like this one, the more I realized how difficult it would be to find a Haitian orphanage director whose heart was in the right place. I planned to hire a Haitian orphanage director to run the day-to-day operations of the house and to run the ministry from the ground in Haiti. I also wanted our director to be Haitian so the kids could fully grow up in their culture. The children would end up being Americanized if Americans raised them. For months I prayed God would provide the right person. I did not want a director who merely saw working at Kingdom Kids Home as a means to a steady income. I wanted someone who felt called to run an orphanage. I prayed God would provide someone who believed he was put on this earth

A Divine Meeting

to take care of the children and to teach them about the Lord. I suspected it would not be an easy find, but I prayed God would plop the right person right into my lap.

Robinson arrived at Tommy's house, and we prepared to head out and walk over to the desolated orphanage. I briefly met Robinson, and the moment I shook his hand a weird feeling came over me. I had barely said two words to the guy, but I remember thinking, Wow, I really like him and having an automatic good feeling about him.

We all walked to shack this man called an orphanage, and my heart broke for what I saw. When we walked up, the kids were hardly clothed. Most were not wearing anything at all. The "house" was filled with about 25 kids who were skinny and sickly. I had imagined the so-called "house" they lived in to be bad, but it was even worse than I could have pictured. There were three slabs of concrete for walls, some boards above them they considered a roof, and no beds. There were a few bunk bed frames, but no mattresses on them. That meant these children were sleeping on the concrete floor each night.

I could not believe it. We stayed and played with this group of children for about an hour. Some got up and danced with us, while others just looked dazed, confused, and unresponsive … probably due to a lack of food. These children defined the "least of these."

As we were walking back from the desolated concrete structure where all those little children lived, I was talking with Robinson. He was fired up and angry that those innocent children were stuck living in that horrible situation and was frustrated there was nothing he could do about it. Tommy and Robinson were trying to turn this corrupt orphanage and the man in charge in to the Haitian Government, but the government could also be corrupt and was not doing much to help the situation.

As Robinson was venting to me on the walk back, I could see he was very passionate about reaching children. God spoke to me and said, "Kristie, ask Robinson to be involved in the orphanage." I thought to myself, No way! That would be totally weird…. I just met the guy an hour ago! He does not know me. I do not really know him. No, not doing it. Then I remembered what I had read on the plane. I remembered the quote that said, "If you do not have confidence and believe in your dream, then no one else will." I knew this was the time for me to have confidence in my God-given dream. If I did not say something and take this shot, I may miss out on a major opportunity, and I may never see Robinson again. In that pivotal moment, I chose to obey. I decided to talk about the orphanage to Robinson.

As I reflect on this part of my story, I realize how important it was for me to obey God in that moment. The remainder of this book would look a lot different or might not exist if I had not listened to God and obeyed what He asked me to do in that moment. Through out the Bible, there are many moments where great men and women had to choose to obey God—and their obedience changed the game for their life and the lives of those around them.

For example, God asks Noah to build an ark to save the human race. Noah chooses to obey and boom! People like you and me are still living on earth today because of Noah's obedience.

God asks Moses to deliver His people out of Egypt. Moses chooses to obey God and goes against Pharaoh, the most powerful leader in that day, leading the Israelites out of slavery. He chooses to obey in spite of his fears, and boom, a whole race of people are delivered.

God asks Nehemiah to restore the city of Jerusalem. Nehemiah chooses to obey even though he was not sure how he'd go about it, and boom, an entire city and its people are restored.

Jesus chooses to obey God and be put to death in the most excruciating way possible, and boom, people's sins can be forgiven, and they have the chance to spend eternity with the Savior.

My point is, great things happen when people choose to obey God. Looking back, I am so grateful I chose to obey in God in that moment. I said to Robinson, "So, Robinson, if you and Tommy do get these kids rescued, where are they going to go?" He said, "We will try to reconnect them with their families, but that will be extremely hard to do. So if we cannot do that, we will place them in good orphanages throughout the area." After he said this, I said, "Well, you know I'm down here in Haiti because I um, want to, um, start and orphanage here. Is that something you may want to be involved in?"

I was so nervous! Right after I asked that, I remember thinking, Oh no, what did I just do? I was ready for him to say, "You want to start an orphanage? How old are you, 21? What can you do? Where are you going to put it? Do you have the money?" I braced myself to hear a bunch of questions I did not have the answers to. Instead, much to my surprise, Robinson just shrugged his shoulders and vaguely said, "Yeah." I took that answer and ran with it! I started to tell him about what I wanted to do, and as I was talking he stopped me and said, "Wait, is this a Christian orphanage? Are you a Christian? Is this going to be a Christian thing?" I said, "Oh, absolutely! That is the whole point! I want to take kids in who do not know the Lord at all and first, build a foundation of faith in their hearts and introduce them to who Jesus is. After they have an understanding of who Jesus is, I want to use this home as a discipleship program. I want to teach and train these children how to do hands on ministry. I want to teach them how to pray for someone, how to share their testimonies, and how to lead others in the prayer of salvation. These kids are going to be the ones to grow up and change their nation for Jesus Christ, not me or an American missions team that's in Haiti for a week. I want to raise up these children to be the next generation of leaders in Haiti." Robinson had a surprised look on his face. He looked at me and said, "That is my dream. My whole life I have felt called to have an orphanage just like the one you are describing. People come to me all the time asking me to help them start an orphanage, but I always say no. They all want to help children, but they leave Jesus out of their plan. Your whole vision is centered around Jesus, so I want to help you. I am in."

Now, I was the one with the surprised look on my face! I sat down with Robinson briefly and showed him some vision sheets I had made for the house and my ministry. He loved the direction I was heading and the goals for Kingdom Kids Homes. He kept reiterating how much he wanted to help me. I said to him, "Robinson, I am only here for a week, and I really need to find somewhere to put this house while I am down here. Do you know of any good pieces of land we could look at?" He knew of a few places and made a couple calls on my behalf. We planned to look at them in those next couple of days.

As I left Tommy's house, I was in shock. I remember thinking, Wow, I have only been in Haiti four hours, and I have already made an awesome connection! Looks like God is already beginning to plop things into my lap.

As I reflect on this part of the story, I am still amazed at how God was coordinating and lining everything up behind the scenes. I have learned, that God truly does work for the good of those who love Him. When you love God, seek Him first, and keep Him at the center of your life, He will honor that and will use you to do things beyond your wildest dreams.

Personal Journal Entry from Missions Journal:

June 17, 2014

Hello from Haiti!

After a very long Monday and night at the airport, we have finally made it to Haiti! We are all settled into the hotel and boy, am I so happy to be here!

Yesterday, I met with my contact, Matt, and his friend, Tommy, to visit the very desolated orphanage Matt has been telling me about for months now. This "orphanage" is owned by a greedy Haitian who uses the kids as a way for him to attract American support. Tommy also brought his translator and Haitian friend, Robinson, along. We walked up to the orphanage, but really, it was more like a few concrete walls with a concrete floor. There were 24 little kids inside and only one lady to take care of them, and all of the children were under the age of 11. Most of them were not even clothed when we were walking up. This was definitely the saddest thing I have ever seen. We walked inside, and most of the kids were just sitting there, with blank stares on their face. They were totally neglected and starving not only for food, but also for love. Every kid hung all over me and Miranda. They were so desperate just to be held. These children did not get attention or an education. They basically just sat there all day, existing... well barely existing.

This situation was absolutely horrible and ever since I heard of these kids back in January, I have felt so compelled to do something. Now, after meeting and holding each of them, I feel more compelled than ever. The translator, Robinson, and I started talking on our walk back, and I started to ask him questions about the orphanage. The whole time I was talking to him, God impressed on my heart to ask him to be involved in the orphanage. I thought, Um, I just met this guy. That might be weird. But, then I thought, if I do not have confidence and believe in my own dream, then no one else will. So, I shyly asked if he would ever want to be involved in helping start an orphanage, and he very vaguely said yes. I started to share more about what I felt God was calling me to do, and he asked me if this was going to be a Christian thing. I said oh, "of course!" And I explained to him that I want the kids to know who Jesus is, then disciple and teach them how to go out and reach people for Jesus. He said "oh my gosh, that's my dream!" I actually said "stop" out loud! I was in such shock! Then, I showed him more about the vision for the orphanage and what I wanted it to be all about. He said he loved the mission behind it, and he would love to help me! He said he knew of some places where we could look to buy land. We are planning on to go look at them later this week!

I have a feeling and a peace about Robinson being my main Haitian contact, and I am excited to get to know him more. And, I know if it's the last thing I do, I need to rescue children just like the ones I met yesterday!

Chapter 14:
You Gotta Know Who You Are

The next morning I woke up excited and full of hope. I still could not believe I made such an incredible connection with Robinson right off the bat. I was eager to see what the rest of the week would hold and expectant even better things were to come.

On my second day in Haiti, I was going to visit and tour a well-established and large orphanage I had heard of months before while I was making various connections in Haiti. This home had around 100 children living in it, and they had a school on site. The orphanage director was a nice, American woman named Jennifer. We had exchanged multiple emails before my trip, and I was looking forward to meeting her and hearing about the organization she worked with.

My dad, a close family friend named Karen, a translator, and I all loaded up in a taxi and drove for about an hour. Right when we pulled up and entered the gate of the orphanage, I loved what I saw. The house was big, beautiful and divided into many different sections. There was a playground out front with a few young kids playing on it. Jennifer came out and greeted us. Shortly after, she gave us a tour of the property. I loved seeing the kids' bathrooms, bunk rooms, and play areas. I was taking notes and snapping a lot of pictures as we walked through. As we were touring this home, my mind began to explode with ideas of how I could set up my home. We asked tons of questions, and Jennifer graciously answered all of them. Jennifer also showed us a separate section of the property where they had a school. We peeked into a couple classrooms and saw the most adorable dark children all dressed in matching uniforms. My imagination was running wild as I dreamed of having my own property where kids would run around playing and laughing.

After we saw the entire property, asked nearly a million questions, and learned a plethora of valuable information, our group, Jennifer, and her husband sat down in their office area to talk. I had some questions I wanted to ask Jennifer about the daily functions of running a children's home. Once I was done, Jennifer asked me an interesting question, which caught me off guard. She looked pretty serious and said, "Kristie, I just do not understand why you want to start you own organization and your own children's home. There are so many awesome organizations already up and running that you could be apart of. Why don't you just join up with one of those instead of starting your own?" I was surprised she said this, especially after she seemed supportive of the idea throughout the tour.

A Divine Meeting

I said, "I don't know. I know starting my own organization from the ground up will be a lot more complicated than just joining one, but all I know is it is what God's calling me to do." At that answer, Jennifer and her husband both proceeded to tell me all the difficulties I would face and all the odds I would have to beat in order to start my own home in Haiti. It did not take me long to realize they were trying to talk me out of starting Kingdom Kids Homes. They explained how hard it would be for an American to work with the Haitian government, that I was a girl and a very young girl at that. Essentially, it would be very tough and highly unlikely for me to establish, run, and maintain a successful organization in Haiti. Jennifer even went as far as to say her time as the orphanage director of her home was almost up and she could put in a recommendation to her boss for me to be the next director there.

My stomach started to hurt when she suggested the idea to me. Every time I know something is not right or I know something is a bad idea, I always get this weird, restless feeling in the pit of my stomach…and I was experiencing it throughout our conversation…big time!

I was shocked Jennifer and her husband were trying to talk me out of starting Kingdom Kids Homes, but I was not offended. I knew they were right. It would be extremely tough and really rare for a young girl like me to be able to beat the odds by starting an orphanage and a brand new organization in Haiti. There would be a lot of challenges I would face, a lot of difficult decisions, and a lot of obstacles I would have to overcome. This couple had been living on they ground in Haiti for about two years. They knew Haiti, and they knew the challenges that came with this type of work. But, they did not know the vision God had put on my heart on January 3, 2012 and the call God had put on my life.

I then realized why God had put me through two years of "prep time." I wanted to rush into things and go back to Haiti during the summer of 2013, but God knew my heart would not be ready. He knew I needed two years to seek Him for direction and to let Him build and define the vision of Kingdom Kids Homes clearly in my heart.

Since I "took the stairs" and had God hammer out the vision in my heart for two years, I was not confused on what God wanted me to do. I knew God wanted me to start an organization called Kingdom Kids Homes and it would be one where kids were brought into the kingdom of God and taught how to bring others into the same kingdom. I knew He wanted me to raise up my kids to be disciples, to teach them how to do hands on ministry, and how to reach people for Jesus. I knew exactly what God's vision was for this ministry He had called me to start. Because of that, I was not even tempted to wavier in the plan or to switch things up because a woman who knew me for an hour was suggesting I do so.

Jennifer was not trying to be mean, she was trying to being honest. I was thankful she shared her concerns, and to be honest, I was discouraged for a few hours after our meeting. Then, I remembered she was just one person with one opinion. Joe had been too. I decided I was not going to let her concerns bring me down or steer me off course because I clearly knew my call, and I knew who I was in Christ.

Over the course of my life, I have realized how essential it is for any believer to know who they are in Christ. I remember being in high school and being tempted to go with the "cool" crowd just to be considered popular. But, then I remembered and knew who I was in Christ, and I realized that doing the right thing and taking the high road was the cool thing to do. It's the same thing when you have a God-given dream. You have to know what God says about you and the vision He has for your life. People will tell you to go to a certain school or to take a certain career path because it will lead to a comfortable lifestyle. But, what is God leading you to do? When you know who you are in Christ, His opinion of you and His plans for your life are the only things that matter. You won't be tempted to change your course when different people share their opinions and thoughts because you will only be concerned with staying on the course God has laid out for you.

Think about Shadrach, Meshach, and Abednego. These men knew who they were in God's eyes. In their day, it was a law for everyone to worship the idols their king, King Nebuchadnezzar, had set up. These three men did not care about what was right in the eyes of society. They refused to worship anything other than God. They knew who they were in the eyes of the Lord and were secure in their relationship with God Most High. These three men were not about to let worldly consequences convince them to do the wrong thing, even if it meant the three of them would be thrown into a fiery furnace. They found their strength and their identity in the Lord.

When Shadrach, Meshach, and Abednego did not bow down, they were thrown into the blazing furnace. Even when they were facing death, they did not give in and did what was right. These men allowed their fear and reverence for the Lord to triumph over any fear man tried to put in their way. Because Shadrach, Meshach, and Abednego honored God, He showed up, was with them in the furnace, and they came out alive, without even the smell of smoke on them. These three men knew who they were in Christ. They stood up for what they believed in, and because of their faith, King Nebuchadnezzar made a new law that everyone in the nation would worship the God of Shadrach, Meshach, and Abednego. The obedience of these three men ended up leading an entire nation to worship God.

When we know who we are in Christ, we won't be swayed to the left or to the right by what the world says. When someone has a different opinion than us or thinks what God has called you to do is an impossible task, we won't panic and switch our plans just because a person thinks we cannot do it.

Get into the Word, and find out who you truly are in Christ. Begin to see yourself as God sees you. You will know what God thinks about you. You will know whom your hope is in. You will base your identity off of words God has spoken to you and not what people have said you should do. It is so important to seek God first and to continuously press into Him throughout the entire journey of following a God-given dream. When you are constantly seeking and asking God for direction, your mind will be so consumed and full of what He is telling you to do that you won't have any room left to consider the opinions of others.

Thankfully, that was the case for me when I met with Jennifer that afternoon in Haiti. I knew exactly what God wanted me to do, and my heart and mind were filled with ideas and directions that came straight from Him. I had no idea how it was going to come about, and I did not know the details. But I chose to trust in what God had been speaking and directing me to do for years now.

Would joining up with Jennifer's organization have been easier? Definitely! Would it have been the more safe and secure path? For sure! But when has any great man or woman of God in the Bible taken the safe or secure path when following after God's plan? Did David stop and ask if going up against a nine foot giant would be safe and secure? The great men and women of the Bible obeyed God with unwavering and unhindered faith, despite their challenges and fears.

When you want to do big things in the kingdom of God, you cannot stick with what is safe and what is secure. There will be fears, challenges, and scary moments, But, when you stick to God's plan, and when you know who you are in Christ, there is no way you will lose.

Personal Journal Entry:

A Prayer Written the Week before the Haiti 2014 Trip
June 9th, 2014

Dear God,

I thank You that You are for me and You are in control of every area of my life. I thank You for knowing me and knowing what is best for me even when I do not understand. Your goodness never ceases to amaze me. I pray Your love captivates my heart and controls every part of it. I thank You for knowing my needs, especially as I prepare to leave for Haiti in a week. God, I thank you for the opportunity to go and for the God-sized vision you have given me. Lord, I pray for an impactful week and that I can tie up a lot of loose ends. I want to specifically pray that we are able to secure a spot to put the orphanage. I pray You give us favor and open doors that need to be opened and shut doors that need to be shut. I pray You give me Your wisdom when I am making decisions, and I pray You show me specific people I need to work with to make this dream a reality. Help me to have boldness and confidence when sharing my vision with others, and I pray the right people will catch hold of the vision.

God, this week is huge, and all of this is way beyond me, but, I thank You for being my strength where I am weak. I am fully trusting in You. I thank You for using me to advance Your kingdom. I love You, Lord. Always use me to do things beyond myself, and always give me God-sized dreams.

In Jesus Name,
Amen.

Chapter 15:
Things Just Got Real

The next morning, Robinson picked up my dad and me from our hotel. We were headed out to look at a piece of land. During my morning quiet time with the Lord, I prayed God would give me clarity as I went about that day. I only had a few more days in Haiti and absolutely no time to waste. I wanted to know right away if the land we were about to look at was the place where God wanted us to build Kingdom Kids Home. I prayed God would be with me as I went out and for the Holy Spirit to give me a clear yes or no on what move I was or was not supposed to make.

While we in the car, Robinson started to share details about this land with me. He told me he was a friend of the man who owned it, and he was a trustworthy guy. He also thought it was enough space to build an orphanage on, and it was located in a safe and quiet neighborhood in Bon Repos, Haiti, which is a city right outside of Port Au Prince. I liked what I was hearing and thought it sounded like a promising spot. Then, Robinson said, "I also have this guesthouse I would like to show you. I own it, and it is right around the corner from the land we are going to look at. I use it as a place for American missionaries to stay while they are in town." He went on to share more details about the guesthouse, and as he was talking, the still small voice of God began to speak to my heart. I heard God say, "Kristie, ask Robinson to use the guest house for the orphanage." There He went again, telling me to ask for some pretty big things that were way out of my comfort zone. Sitting in the passenger seat, I silently began to converse with God—"Um, no! I can't say that! That's a huge thing to ask someone. I would be asking him to give up his house and his side business he started. No way."

Then, Robinson said, "When I first bought this house, the whole reason I bought it was because I felt God calling me to use it for some kind of ministry, but that dream kind of fell through. Now I am just using it as a guesthouse." Once Robinson said that, I gained some courage. Again, I thought of the saying I read on the plane—"If you do not have confidence and believe in your dream, then no one else will."

I knew this was yet another moment, and I had to obey God and believe in the dream He had given me. I said, "Okay Robinson…the whole time you have been talking, God has been putting an idea on my heart. What if we use the guesthouse for the orphanage? What if we make the necessary renovations and improvements and then start the home there? What would you think of that?"

Just like the first time I asked him a big question, Robinson gave another vague response. He just simply shrugged his shoulders and said, "I would like that." Right when Robinson said those four words, the still small voice of God spoke to my heart again and said, "That's it. That is where you are going to put Kingdom Kids Home." I turned my head to look out the passenger window so Robison could not see the tears forming in my eyes. My heart leaped for joy, and even though I had not laid eyes on the house, I knew I had heard clearly from God and we had found our spot.

Shortly after that conversation, we pulled up to the land. The moment we pulled up I started to feel an uneasy feeling, the one I always get in my stomach when I do not have peace about a situation. I had not even made it out of the car and God was already giving me clarity. I still talked the owner for a few minutes and surveyed the property. Nothing was wrong. It was a good size piece of land and the neighborhood appeared to be safe and quiet. It was a nice piece of property, but I knew it was not for us. As Robinson was conversing with the owner, I told my dad the land was definitely not the one, and we needed to go look at the guesthouse. My dad looked surprised and said, "Are you sure?" I know he was probably concerned I was about to say no to a solid option because I was putting all my hope in the guesthouse. I let him know, "Dad, beyond the shadow of doubt this is what we are supposed to do." He asked me, "Wow. Are you sure you are not just excited about the guesthouse possibility?" If I had been my dad in that situation, I would have been asking the same questions. Normally, I would have been more hesitant and not as confident in my decision, but I knew what I heard in the car was the Lord speaking and not at all my own thoughts. I said, "Dad, God spoke to me in the car and told me the guesthouse is where we are supposed to put Kingdom Kids Home." Again, he looked surprised and said, "Okay, lets go look at the guesthouse." I am beyond grateful my dad did not question my judgment in that moment, but trusted I had heard from God. That was enough of an answer for him.

I explained to Robinson that I did not have a peace about this land, but I wanted to see the guesthouse. I said, "Robinson, this land is great, but I know this is not it. But, when you were talking about the guesthouse in the car, the Holy Spirit gave me a lot of peace about that option, and I feel we need to go after that." He said, "Okay sister, but we need to pray about this first." I laughed and said, "I know! I am not making any big moves without involving the Lord, but I believe this is what He has for us." And with that, we loaded back into the car and drove over to the guesthouse, which was just 3 blocks away.

As we pulled up to the house, I noticed right away how perfect it would be for an orphanage. It already had a retention wall around the property, a gate, and a security watchtower. All of these things were essential security measures for an orphanage to have, and this house already had them in place. As we came through the gate, the entirety of the house came into my view for the first time. As we drove in, an overwhelming sense of peace came over me. We began to walk through the house, and I was amazed by what I saw. As we walked through each room, I could not help the tears falling from my eyes. The house was perfect. It was the perfect size and had large rooms inside that would be perfect for kids' bunk rooms. As we were touring the house, the Holy Spirit kept whispering to my heart, "This is it." Not to mention that during my years of "prep time," God had shown me a picture of what the house was supposed to look like. As we were walking through Robinson's house, I could not help but notice how similar the house looked to the sketch I had drawn up years before. It was not exact, but it was extremely close to what God showed me the house would look like. It was just more confirmations that Robinson's house was the right place.

We sat on the back patio of the house, and Robinson and I talked for about an hour. I shared with him all the crazy doors God had opened and all the ways He had provided for me and this vision over the past few years.

After hearing my story, Robinson said, "Wow, sister! I can see this is a God thing and not just you. My faith is growing just from hearing your story. You know, when I first bought this house, the whole reason I bought it was because I felt God calling me to have an orphanage here. I started to plan for it, and I bought two bunk beds, but then I realized I could never keep up an orphanage and take care of my family. So, I put that dream on hold, and I have been using this house as a guesthouse in the meantime. But, I think God has brought you and me together so we can reach our God-given dream together and start an orphanage to rescue children and teach them about Jesus Christ."

I was in shock. As I write this, I am still in awe of how God was working everything out behind the scenes. He was prepping Robinson's heart and grooming it to be an orphanage director when the right time came. When I mentioned the idea of having the orphanage at the guesthouse, that was not the first time the idea had crossed Robinson's mind. God had already gotten him ready long before he met me.

With tears in my eyes I said, "Robinson, I think you are right. I do not feel called to live in Haiti and run this home, so for years I have prayed God would put the right person across my path to run this house. That is the most important part. I could dream up the home to be a certain way and for the children to be discipled and for them to grow in their relationship with God everyday, but if the person running the day-to-day operations is not doing that, what's the point? The person running this house needs to have a vision that is aligned with mine, and you do. You are the leader I have been praying about for years. You are the person God has put across my path to run this house. I want you to be the orphanage director."

Robinson's face lit up when I said this. I don't think he realized I was not planning on living in Haiti. He said, "Wow! That is my dream! I have always dreamed of running and overseeing an orphanage! Before I say yes, I have to ask my wife! But I know she is going to be so excited because it has always been her dream to have an orphanage too! Then, I have to pray and get the final word from God this is what I am supposed to do, but I am 99 percent sure it is, sister! I am so excited! But, I just have to pray and get final confirmation from God first." I told him, "That is okay! Take your time. I know God is not going to give me a yes and you a no if we are serving the same God!"

Soon after our conversation, Robinson drove my dad and I back to our hotel. The whole ride back, I was in a state of disbelief, and I am pretty sure my dad was too. Robinson dropped us off and promised me he would pray about everything and get in touch with me soon. My dad and I walked into the hotel lobby and realized the team was not back yet. We stopped in the lobby for a moment to catch our breath. I said, "Dad! What on earth just happened?!" I had held my composure pretty well the entire time I was with Robinson, but the moment my dad and I were alone, the tears began to fall hard. As I was crying happy tears in my dad's arms, I could hardly get my words out. Through the sobs I explained to my dad why I was so amazed. I said, "Dad…about a week before this trip, I prayed a bold prayer for God to just give us the land…and it looks like that is exactly what He just did! I cannot believe that!" It was true! Since Robinson owned the property, we just avoided about seven steps we would have had to go through to purchase land, and we saved a ton of money. In one day it looked like God had plopped the property and the director right into my lap, just like I prayed He would.

One of my favorite verses in the Bible is 1 Corinthians 2:9: "No eye has seen, no ear has heard, and no mind has imagined what God has prepared for those who love him." (NLT). When we love God and do our best to honor Him and obey Him, there is no telling what he will do through our lives! He will use you and do things through your life that will blow your mind!

My mind was blown that day in Haiti when I discovered Robinson had the house we were going to use for Kingdom Kids Home and he was going to be the orphanage director. As I look back on the journey, I have learned that when you are going after a dream God has put on your heart, it is so important to obey what He is asking you to do and to keep your eyes focused on Jesus every step of the way. You have to trust God and keep your faith in Him, even when circumstances are dim. This reminds me of when Peter was attempting to walk on water in order to meet Jesus. Jesus commanded him to get out of the boat and to walk on the water. Peter believed he could do it and wanted to obey what Jesus was asking him to do. He had enough courage to get out of the boat and to start moving towards Jesus. That is step one. First, we have to choose to obey what God is calling us to do and take our first few steps forward. We need to choose to "get out of the boat" and follow the dream God has placed on our heart.

Once Peter got out of the boat and started to walk on the water, he noticed the uncertain and scary circumstances around him and began to lose hope. He took his eyes off Jesus and quickly began to sink. Secondly, when we begin to go after the dreams God has placed on our hearts, we cannot let scary situations, doubt, and disbelief allow us to sink. Even though people and circumstances will come against us, we have to keep your eyes on Jesus and on what He is leading us to do every step of the way. Follow after his voice and keep your heart and mind centered on Him. Peter had enough courage to start walking, but fell shortly after the first challenge came. We need to keep our eyes fixed on Christ, despite challenges or obstacles, and we will reach the destination He is calling us to.

As I write this chapter, two years after the day we found the home, I still cannot believe how God provided for me that day. It was truly a miracle. All along, God saw me. He knew my heart and had heard my every prayer. He had me in the palm of His hand. After that day, the dream God had placed on my heart two years before did not seem like a far off and distant idea. All of the sudden it felt close and tangible. Just like that, the dream in my mind started to shift into reality. I knew I was on my way. Things had just got real.

Personal Journal Entry from Missions Journal:

June 19th, 2014

WOW! Today was crazy!

 This morning, instead of going out to the Pastor's Conference with the rest of the team, my dad and I went with Robinson to look at a potential piece of land to put the orphanage. When we were driving to the land, Robinson began to tell me about this guesthouse he owns and how it is a place he uses for American missionaries to stay. As he was talking about the guesthouse, God put on my heart the idea of using the guest house as the orphanage. Initially, *I thought,* I cannot do that…it's Robinson's house and the way he makes money! But, then Robinson said something about using the guesthouse for another purpose and I jumped at that opportunity! I said, "I feel like the Lord has been putting on my heart that we use the guest house for the orphanage." Robinson said, "I would like that" to the idea of using the guest house for the orphanage and right when he said yes to the possibility, God spoke to me and said, "This is it Kristie. That is the spot." I got so excited I had to hold back my tears and play it cool until we actually saw the house!

 First, we went to the piece of land we were originally supposed to look at, and it was nice. But, right when we pulled up, I got a clear "no" from the Holy Spirit. I told Robinson I was feeling a peace about the guesthouse, so we went to see it. It was perfect. Right when we pulled up, I had tears in my eyes because I just knew that was it. We toured the house, and it was already pretty nice. I was thinking of all the little changes we'd have to make, but it was great and in a very safe neighborhood. Also, there was a great Christian school located around the corner and up the road. Then, Robinson and I sat down and talked for two hours about our dreams and what we would like to see happen with the place if we made it into the first Kingdom Kids Home. After I shared my heart with him and told him how God had been working everything out so far, he said he felt peace about the entire idea and he could tell it was a God thing. He said he was going to pray about it and get the final confirmation from God that this is what he was supposed to do. So, I am still waiting on that, but I am 99 percent sure that today we found the place where the future Kingdom Kids Home will be! I cannot believe it!

Chapter 16:

The Cat is All The Way Out of The Bag

The next morning, my friends and I were eating breakfast with the team before going out for another day of ministry. Over breakfast, I was filling my friends in on the exciting discovery. They were so excited for me and anxious to see what would happen next, just like I was!

I broke away from breakfast for a moment to check my email in the lobby. (It was the only place we could get Wi-Fi.) When I opened my inbox, I saw that Robinson had sent me an email. I eagerly opened it. It read:

> *Hallelujah! I woke up this morning and feel wonderful! Because I know for sure now God wants me to say yes to you and to our wonderful and great sense of dreams, to serve, to help and support with love and respect.*
>
> *I pray and believe that God will give to us the extra energy to defend the weak and the fatherless; uphold the cause of the poor and the oppressed.*

God told me it's the right time now to open my door to some orphans. I will follow His direction and His instruction, and together sister, we will give to the orphans a place where they can be directed and supervised, loved and nurtured for the kingdom of God.

Yes, sister, let's go forward and make it happen in the name of God.

Thanks

I will not leave you as orphans; I will come to you.
John 14:18

May God bless you
Robinson

Immediately, my heart became overwhelmed with excitement. I said, "Oh my gosh!" and literally started jumping up and down. People watching me probably thought I had just won the lottery, and honestly, I felt like I had. I was surprised I received an answer back from Robinson so quickly, but at the same time, I was not. God had opened up every door and plopped everything I needed in my lap up to this point, and He was just continuing to do so! I was amazed, pumped, and beyond excited. It was official. We had the house and the orphanage director for Kingdom Kids Home, and God worked in mind-blowing ways to get us there.

I ran back into the breakfast room to share the news. With tears in my eyes and a huge smile on my face, I told my friends we had found the spot for Kingdom Kids Home. Robinson had said yes! They all screamed with excitement and after lots of celebratory hugs, I raced to find my dad so I could tell him the news. When I found him, I said, "Dad, we did it! It's official! Robison said he's in!" My dad and I rejoiced together. We both knew only God could have worked the situation out the way He did.

As I write this today, two years after receiving the big news, I am still in awe of God's goodness. He is a miracle working God, and I will forever be grateful for the way He worked out this miracle in my life.

The next day, my dad and I went back and started to take measurements of the house and talk renovations with Robinson. It was fun to dream and plan all the changes we could make to turn this guesthouse in to the best children's home it could be. Talking logistics always brings reality into an exciting situation. But, I was not going to let all the plans we had to make, all the legal steps we would have to go through, and all the money we would have to raise ruin my excitement. I knew we had a long road ahead of us, but God was clearly in everything I was setting my hand to, and I was confident He would make the path smooth.

That night, Daniel had me share the miraculous testimony of finding the house and Robinson with the whole missions team. This time, when I was sharing my dream with the 65 plus team of missionaries, I felt confident in sharing the vision God had put on my heart. I had shared it with only a select few people before, but it was easier to share it this time because it was now a real thing! I was no longer sharing it in faith. It was happening! Everyone was amazed at the miraculous story, and at the end, they took up an offering to help me get started in launching the home and ministry. In just one night, I had raised just over $1,300! God was already providing the funds, and He was already making the way... just like He promised He would.

I left Haiti a few days later promising Robinson I would return in December for a business/ planning type of trip. Since I was going into my senior year of college, I could not just come down to visit Haiti anytime I pleased. I planned on waiting till my Christmas break to come back, but in those next five months I would be busy launching the ministry, raising support, making the ministry an official non-profit organization, getting the word out about Kingdom Kids Homes, and launching the website all while starting my senior of college at ORU. Back home, I had a ton of other responsibilities such as, serving as the Head Resident Advisor to a dorm full of girls at ORU, the director of the children's ministry at my church, and being a full time college student. Safe to say, my plate was going to be completely full, but so was my heart. It was full of dreams and ambitions, and even though I knew the upcoming year would be the craziest and busiest year of my life, I was excited and ready for it.

I am taking the time to describe what my life looked at this time not to say "Look at how much I was doing as a senior in college!" but to encourage you to follow the dream God has placed on your heart, despite what season of life you are in. I have heard so many of my friends share their dreams or what they feel God is calling them to do with their lives, and they finish their stories by saying, "But that will be way, way, way down the road. Probably sometime after I am married, with kids, and settled." When I hear this, I try my best to have self-control and to keep my mouth shut, but in my head I am thinking, Why? If you know what God is calling you to do, why do you keep locking it away, waiting to see how your life pans out first? The truth is, life will always be busy. You will always have a lot of things to occupy your time and different priorities to focus on. If you keep pushing your dream off, waiting for a convenient time to show up, chances are you are never going to pursue it because something else will always come up. If your are young, you will use the excuse "I just want to make it through school." Then you will make it through school and say, "Now I just want to get a job that pays well and get married." Then you will do those things and you will say, "Now we just want to figure out life as a married couple and start having children." Finishing school, getting a great job, getting married, and starting a family are all amazing, exciting, and important seasons of life. Personally, part of my dream is to experience each of those seasons and to experience them to the fullest. I am not trying to downplay those moments in our lives and I am not trying to say they are not important. But, I do want to encourage you to not allow the dreams and visions God has placed in the depths of your heart to take a back seat. Before you know it, your life will have slowly passed by and your dreams that were constantly put on hold will never have come to be.

The good news is, it is never too early or too late to start pursuing your God-given dreams. If you are a young person reading this, start taking small steps towards your dream that will impact your future in a big way. If you are older, and you are reading this, thinking about how you constantly put your dreams on hold, it is not too late to turn it around and to start pursuing them today. My point is, there will never be a convenient time for us to start pursing our dreams. My senior year of college was clearly jammed packed with things. With the type of schedule I already had, launching a non-profit organization was not an easy thing to throw in the mix, but I knew it was what God had called me to. As I mentioned before, we will have to sacrifice and work hard to reach our God given dreams. Again, "Work as if it depends on you, and pray as if it depends on God." Following your God given dreams will take hard work. It will involve staying up late, sacrificing your personal time and money, and putting yourself out there. It will not be easy or convenient, but it will be so worth it. And believe me, there is no better feeling than running full force after the dreams God has placed on your heart and knowing you are right where he wants you to be.

Once I got back to America, I began working on making Kingdom Kids Homes an official non-profit organization so we could begin taking donations. I was not really sure how the whole process worked. I had never launched a non-profit business before, but thankfully, God provided a great connection to help me with it. For quite a few years, I had been leading a Bible study with a group of eight young girls. These girls were now going into the 7th grade, and I had been discipling and mentoring this group since they were in fifth grade.

The Cat is All The Way Out of The Bag

One of the girls in my group had a dad who was a non-profit lawyer. His entire job was to help people with the legal side of launching a non-profit, which I did not understand at all. I met with him, and he offered to help me with all the legal work for free. On top of that, all the Bible study families surprised me by offering to come together to cover all the fees it took to file for Kingdom Kids Homes to become an official non-profit! I was so blessed by this and saw it as another way God was plopping every need I had into my lap. After we filed, Dan, the non-profit lawyer, informed me it usually took anywhere from 30 to 60 days for the IRS to grant an organization their 501c3 and official non-profit status. He said if it took longer than 60 days, it could take up to two years for the process to be completed, and since we were planning on opening the orphanage that coming summer, we did not have that kind of time! I prayed that God would show His favor and for it to be a quick and easy process. Again, God answered another prayer. It took 35 days for our non-profit to become official. It happened in record time!

Once we were an official non-profit organization and our website was ready, it was time to go full on public with the launch of Kingdom Kids Homes! After keeping this dream secret for such a long time, it was crazy to me. Everyone I knew was about to find out. If it were up to me, I would probably still have kept it secret. But we had to start raising funds, and it would be hard to do that without people knowing about it! During the first week of my senior year of ORU, I got a text asking if I could be a part of a video ORU was making for a chapel service. The video was to showcase people who had attended, graduated, or in my case, were currently attending ORU who were going after big dreams and who were going into every man's world. I was asked if they could show my picture and announce what was happening with Kingdom Kids Homes in the video. This video would be played to the entire student body and would be seen by the ORU community. I read the text thinking, am I really ready for everyone here to know this huge dream? Then I thought, Well it's free advertising and people need to start finding out about it, so might as well go big! So, I was put in the video along with people like, Ryan Tedder (the lead singer of the famous band One Republic), Kari Jobe (a world wide famous worship leader), and Michelle Bachman (a United States Representative). The cat was let way out the bag, and everyone found out about the orphanage I was planning to start. In the lobby after chapel, multiple people came up to me with surprised looks on their faces, saying, "I had no idea you were doing that!"

In the following weeks, we launched our website, all our social media, and more people were finding out about Kingdom Kids Homes. Even though it was exciting, it was also weird to have people know about this big dream that was so precious, delicate, and near to my heart. It was also a lot of pressure because even though I had the house, the director, and the organization, I did not have the thousands and thousands of dollars it would take to create this home. I was fully moving forward in faith, trusting and believing God would provide every last dollar I needed to create the first Kingdom

Kids Home. He had brought me this far and had already plopped so many things into my lap, I knew He would not stop now.

I had a lot of money to raise in a seven month span. I was meeting with people, applying for funds, and working on mustering up all the financial support I could, but at the end of the day, I knew that would not be enough. I knew I had to trust God to make the way, just like He had done through this entire journey.

This reminds me of the story in the Bible when Moses was leading the Israelites out of Egypt. Moses did not have every step of their journey mapped out, but he was following God's direction and trusting God to lead him in the right direction. Things were looking good, until the Israelites came to the shores of the Red Sea and saw the Egyptians were hot on their tales. When the Israelites turned around and saw the Egyptians pursing them and when they looked ahead and saw the enormous Red Sea in front of them, they began to lose faith and they started to panic. They started to blame Moses saying he brought them in the wilderness just to die. In this type of scenario, you would think Moses would be panicking and he would start apologizing profusely for bringing the group to a dead end. But, instead, here is how Moses responded in this moment of panic. He said, "Do not be afraid. Stand firm and you will see the deliverance the Lord will bring you today. The Egyptians you see today you will never see again. The Lord will fight for you; you need only to be still" (Exodus 14:13-14, NIV). Moses' reaction here astounds and inspires me. Death was staring him in the face, but he still had faith in God and chose to trust the Lord would take care of him and the Israelites. That is exactly what the Lord did. He gave Moses instruction to place his staff into the water, and when he did, the sea parted and the Israelites were able to walk through on dry ground. They all made it safely to the other side, while the Egyptians drowned.

When you are following after God's dream for your life but facing what seems like an impossible situation, react like Moses. You need to say that even though I do not know how this vision is going to work out, I know it is from the Lord, and I know that as I do my best to follow after it and obey him, He will fight for me. He will take care of me. He will not leave me, and with Him, I will reach my destination.

Even though I had a long road of raising funds and making big plans in front of me, I knew my God was on my side, and I knew my God would fight for me. I knew God had not brought me that far to leave me now. My faith and hope was fully in Him. And, as usual, my God did not let me down.

Personal Journal Entry:

August 25th, 2014

Dear Journal,

I have some news for you... Kingdom Kids Home is happening! It's crazy to read back on my old journal entries and watch how God was always orchestrating every piece together!

My trip to Haiti could not have gone better! We found the location for the home, an incredible orphanage director, made amazing connections, and now...we're doing this! Kingdom Kids Home is not just a far off dream anymore! In fact, it's actually very alive! So alive that we are going public with it later today when we launch all our website and all our social media. The cat will be fully let out of the bag, and my whole world will know! The cat was already released at ORU when they showed a picture of me in a slideshow with all these ORU alumni who had reached their dreams and who had done big things with their lives. And, there was me. I was up on the big screen right next to Kari Jobe and Ryan Tedder! So crazy! Everyone at school has been coming up to me, asking a ton of questions... even people I barely know. It's funny because I am so normal. It's weird. Everyone at my school knows a secret dream that has been hidden in my heart for such a long time. It feels like they've read my diary! But, I am glad people *know so later today won't be such a shock for them. I am excited to share it with the world but also nervous because this dream is so precious to me. But, if we want to raise money, everyone is going to have to find out sometime!*

It is an amazing but strange feeling seeing your dream come to life. If this journey has taught me one thing, it is how small and insignificant I am, and how big and powerful my God is. He truly has plopped everything I have needed right into my lap. It is the most humbling thing to have God work through you to do something way beyond yourself. This entire story is such a testimony to the faithfulness of God. There is truly nothing He cannot do! I know He will make a way and provide every last dollar we need to see this home through.

I cannot believe Kingdom Kids Homes is going public in a few hours. I feel like a kid on Christmas Eve!

Chapter 17:
What Faith Can Do

Growing up, I admired people who launched their own ministries who were fully living out what God had created them to do. Before I knew it, things were off and running and just like that, as a 21-year-old senior in college, I had a ministry of my own. It felt too good to be true. During breaks between classes, I would have phone calls from my dorm room with builders, pastors, filmmakers, businessmen, and different ministry connections sharing the plan of Kingdom Kids Home with them, praying they would catch the vision.

My senior year was nothing short of crazy, and looking back now, I am not sure how I did it. I was constantly working on either things for school, church, Kingdom Kids Homes, or my head resident advisor position. I would be up late working on ministry things, then I would wake up at 5:30 a.m., go to the closest Panera Bread at 6:00 a.m., write a paper, then go to my class at 9:50 a.m. and turn it in! During class, I was constantly working on things and found it extremely hard to pay attention (sorry teachers!)… don't worry, I still got good grades. I would not recommend living that kind of lifestyle, but I knew I was living out what God had for me in that season of my life, and that alone was extremely energizing. I wanted to do everything with excellence, and if my life had to be insane for a short season in order to do it, that was okay with me.

Christmas break came quickly, and two days after Christmas in 2014, I headed back down to Haiti for three short days. This trip was a business trip to get some major things set in stone for the home. We were only there for a few days, but had an extremely packed schedule. During those three days, I would be touring existing orphanages, meeting with lawyers to talk about the legal side of things, interviewing potential house staff members, visiting the church our kids would attend, and meeting with architects and contractors to talk about renovations for the house. We did not have a free minute to spare! The days were long and exhausting, but energizing at the same time. With every completed meeting or appointment, I knew I was one step closer to reaching my destination, and that truth kept me going.

Even though this trip was short, I learned a lot about myself and about running a ministry. I had no experience in starting a children's home and overseeing an organization, and as I previously mentioned, before I knew it, I was running my own! I was doing the best I could, putting my plans into action, while following the voice of the Lord, and learning as I went. On this trip I learned how to be a confident and bold leader. Not confident in an egotistical way, thinking my way was the only and best way. But, confident in a way where I knew what God was calling me to do, and I was not going to let anyone sway me off course or take advantage of me.

I love the quote President Theodore Roosevelt said. I say it to myself all the time when I am facing a tough situation in leadership. He said, "Speak softly and carry a big stick; you will go far." Here, Teddy Roosevelt was encouraging people to strive for peace and to make it their goal to get along with everyone, but to stick up for themselves and what they believe is right when necessary. This is a huge lesson I have learned through the entire journey of launching Kingdom Kids Homes, and I still remind myself of it today. Our goal should be to love everyone and to live in harmony with one another, but when someone is trying to change your plans, run your organization, or attempting to walk all over you, you need to stick up for yourself and protect what you strongly believe in.

For example, the most exhausting day of the December trip was the day I sat down with Robinson and his lawyer to talk about the legal contract for renting Robinson's house. First off, just writing the words legal contract sounds boring to me! Do not worry, I will not go into detail of what the contract said, but let me tell you, legal work is something I am not passionate about in life! I knew it had to be done and the issues had to be talked through, but I was already dreading the day before it had even begun. I sat down with my dad, Robinson, and his lawyer to talk through and put on paper the conditions of Kingdom Kids Homes renting the house.

To sum up our meeting, Robinson's lawyer was not being fair and wanted Kingdom Kids Homes to pay for a lot more than we should have been paying for. He kept insisting and telling Robinson to raise the price of the rent. (Robinson continuously refused, which allowed me to trust him even more). His lawyer wanted us to pay monthly for things around the house that was not a renter's responsibility. Since we were Americans, he was trying to take advantage of us and make us pay way more money than we should have been.

As I have said before, I did not know what I was doing. I had never been in a situation like this. I had not even rented my first apartment. I was only a college student. Since I had no experience in this area, I did not have much confidence in what I thought was right or fair. But, I had done my homework. I knew what other ministries were paying to rent there facilities, and I had examples of their legal contracts with me. In that meeting, I do not know what came over me, but when his lawyer was coming against me, I felt extremely brave and confident. Okay, I do know what came over me… it was the Holy Spirit. He gave me the courage I needed to "carry a big stick" and to stick up for what I felt was right in the middle of a tense conversation. He made me brave, and He gave me the words to say. I am proud to say I walked away from that meeting with the odds in my favor. We walked away with fair terms, conditions, and prices set in stone.

God gave me the confidence I needed to stick up for what I felt was right and, like always, He was my strength in an area where I was weak.

That is just what our God does. When we give Him the tiniest bit of faith, and move forward, following after Him with the little bit of courage we have, He will come through for us… every single time. As I write this, again I am reminded of the woman in the Bible who had the issue of blood. Her story is found in Mark 5:25-34:

> And a woman was there who had been subject to bleeding for twelve years. She had suffered a great deal under the care of many doctors and had spent all she had, yet instead of getting better she grew worse. When she heard about Jesus, she came up behind him in the crowd and touched his cloak, because she thought, "If I just touch his clothes, I will be healed." Immediately her bleeding stopped and she felt in her body that she was freed from her suffering.
>
> At once Jesus realized that power had gone out from him. He turned around in the crowd and asked, "Who touched my clothes?"
>
> "You see the people crowding against you," his disciples answered, "and yet you can ask, 'Who touched me?'"
>
> But Jesus kept looking around to see who had done it. Then the woman, knowing what had happened to her, came and fell at his feet and, trembling with fear, told him the whole truth. He said to her, "Daughter, your faith has healed you. Go in peace and be freed from your suffering." (NIV)

I will always be in awe of the faith this woman carried! She was out of hope and out of options. She had no money and no cure for her disease. Despite everything working against her, she still chose to turn to Jesus. She chose to put her faith, hope, and trust in Him. Where she was weak, He was strong.

I came home from my December trip with the plans drawn and a lot of lose ends tied up. Now, I only had to come up with about $45,000 in less than six months. Sounds easy, right? It seemed like an incredibly large number and a ginormous goal that would be hard to reach since I only had about $1,000 in the bank at that time. But, despite the huge mountain to climb, just like the woman with the issue of blood, I chose to put every ounce of faith I had in my God. I knew He would not have brought me that far to not provided for me in crazy ways.

Yes, I was inexperienced. Yes, I was figuring it all out and learning a lot as I went. Yes, in the eyes of most human beings I would be the least likely candidate to pull something like this off. But, isn't that the kind of person God loves to use? People who have nothing else to work with except full reliance and trust in Him.

One of my favorite authors, Bob Goff, said it best in his book *Love Does*. He said, "God loves the humble ones, and the humble ones often don't make the first round draft picks for the jobs with big titles or positions. But they always seem to be the first round picks for God when he's looking for someone to use in a big way."

> But he said to me, "My grace is sufficient for you, for my power is made perfect in weakness." Therefore I will boast all the more gladly about my weaknesses, so that Christ's power may rest on me. That is why, for Christ's sake, I delight in weaknesses, in insults, in hardships, in

persecutions, in difficulties. For when I am weak, then I am strong.

2 Corinthians 12:9-11, NIV

His grace will cover the areas where you feel weak. Just like the woman with the issue of blood, put your every ounce of faith in Him, and there's no way you can go wrong.

I arrived home from that short December trip on December 30th, 2014. The next day, I went to check the P.O. box for Kingdom Kids Homes, and I found a check inside for $10,000! That check could not have come at a better time. I had just gotten back from a trip where we set the budget and had a firm grasp on the large amount of funds it would take to start this home. It was a large number, and I had only a little amount of money in the bank. This check was the ray of hope I needed. As I stood in the lobby of the post office with tears forming in my eyes, holding the $10,000 check I thought, I can do this!

I prayed "Thank You, God, for seeing me. Thank You for how You are already providing. My faith is in You. I know this is just the beginning of all the doors You are going to open and all the ways You are going to provide."

Personal Journal Entry from My Prayer Journal:

May 13, 2015

> "At my first defense, no one came to my support, but everyone deserted me. May it not be held against them. But the Lord stood at my side and gave me strength, so that through me the message might be fully proclaimed. The Lord will rescue me from every attack and will bring me safely into His heavenly Kingdom. To Him be the glory forever."
>
> 2 Timothy 4:16-18.

God, sometimes I feel like Paul when he was writing this letter to Timothy. Sometimes I feel alone in the journey of Kingdom Kids, and it is hard when people do not come through. If there's one thing I've learned it's that people are not perfect, and they will disappoint you. But, just as Paul says, you are always standing by my side and I know I am never alone. You truly have been and will be my strength when I am feeling weak. I thank You for never leaving me, but You hold me in Your righteous hands. Truly, no one compares to You. Just like the song I used to sing when I was young: "You are my strength when I am weak, you are the treasure that I seek. You are my all in all."

God, I thank you for being with me all through my life. I cannot think of an instance where I needed you and you were not faithful. God, I don't care how crazy, complicated, or tough situations get, You are still my God! The Lord almighty who just simply speaks and the earth melts! There is no problem that is too big for You. There is no amount of money that is too big for You to provide. There is no vision too crazy that You can't help fulfill. Through it all, God, my eyes are on You, and I trust in You.

Lord, You know all our needs. I give them to You, and I trust in You wholeheartedly.

Amen.

Chapter 18:
Dreams Do Come True

The next six months went by in the blink of an eye. Before I knew it, I had graduated from ORU, moved out of the dorms, and started a full-time staff position at my church. It was summer 2015, and it was time for me to open an orphanage… just as the Lord had told me I would. There were so many times during those six months leading up to the opening that I would be driving around in my car just crying. Good tears, of course! They were tears sprung out of the depths of my heart. They were tears full of bewilderment, thankfulness, and deep gratitude. I could not believe God was actually doing this! It was not make believe any more. Kingdom Kids Home was on the cusp of opening its doors to 16 children.

Obtaining the actual 16 children for our house was an arduous process. Robinson and our social worker handled the screening process and sent me the final results. I preferred it to be this way. I did not want to hear about all the children we were turning away because they did not meet some of the certain stipulations we set up for the house.

I remember the day I got the first email from Robinson with pictures and basic info of the first few children we accepted into our house. I was driving in my car when I saw Robinson had emailed me. I immediately pulled over and opened the email to see some of the sweetest faces and to read some of the most heartbreaking stories. Tears flowed from my eyes as I read how Judeline, a three-year-old girl, had a father who passed away and a mother with a mental problem, and due to that, she was in the hospital and not able to take care of Judeline. Even though Judeline was three, she was the size of a one year old in America. She was extremely malnourished and sick. I read about Jeffly, a seven-year-old boy, whose mother died and father abandoned him. He had no one to take care of him so his grandmother temporarily took him in. I read about Jacky, a six-year-old boy, who had no mother and was homeless, sleeping on the streets everyday with his father. I read how Shaianka, a six-year-old girl, became an orphan after both her parents were murdered. I read about Dorval, a six-year-old boy, whose father killed his mother and then left him all alone.

I saw their faces and read each child's story, I prayed and thanked God they now had a home. Little by little and day by day, as I prayed for the children, my love for them grew. After praying for the past few years for the children who would one day be a part of Kingdom Kids Home, it was amazing to be able to pray for each child by name and to picture their faces as I was talking to God. I could not wait to meet the children. I was so in love with them already.

The home was scheduled to open June 28, 2015. The weeks leading up to the trip were insanely busy. I would walk through Hobby Lobby crying as I picked out decorations for the girl's and boy's bunk rooms. I got weird looks from multiple people at Walmart while I walked around pushing two carts filled to the brim with pillows for the kid's beds. I loved shopping for cups the children would drink out of and plates they would eat their meals off of. Shoes, underwear, sheets, towels, toothbrushes, you name it; I guarantee you we had at least 16 of them. And we were bringing it all with us to Kingdom Kids Home!

For our first trip, we took a team of 24 missionaries with us. We would be in Haiti for a full week of ministry. I went through a ridiculous number of emotions during that first mission trip. It was my first time ever taking my own team on a missions trip with Kingdom Kids Homes. Since my first missions trip to Guatemala at age 14, I had dreamed of taking people on trips with my own organization… and I was doing it now!

My family and a few family friends came with me to Haiti a few days before the team arrived. We were going to do last minute work and organization, which needed to be done inside the house before opening day. The day before the team arrived, Robinson and I commissioned our house staff. We all gathered on the back patio of Kingdom Kids Home, and Robinson and I both shared the mission of our house and why it existed. I told the staff the most important part of their job at Kingdom Kids Home was to come alongside our kids to help them truly know Jesus. While Robinson was speaking to the staff, he shared something that caught me totally off guard. He was telling everyone the story of how he and I met and how it was truly a God-ordained relationship. Robinson shared how many people had asked him to help them start an orphanage. He said that every time he would pray and ask God if that was the person he was supposed to partner with, he would get a no from God every single time. God would tell Robinson "No, this is not the person yet," and he would get frustrated. It was his dream to have an orphanage, and he would always plead to God "Why not? why can't I help these people." But on the day he was walking to Tommy's house, on the day he and I met, God spoke to him and said, "Robinson, today is the day. You are going to meet the person who's going to help you start the orphanage."

When I heard Robinson's story, my eyes immediately began to fill with tears. He had never told me that before. It was amazing to hear how God was working on his end and directing him, just as He had directed me on that same day to ask Robinson to be involved. I was blown away to hear how God had orchestrated all the details behind the scenes… but I should not have been surprised! He is God, and that is just what He does. He "plops things in our laps" when we ask Him to.

After Robinson spoke, we laid hands on our staff and prayed for them. We commissioned each of them not as staff members, but as missionaries to each of our kids at Kingdom Kids Home. I shared with them a quote by Ann Voskamp, which says: "Your most meaningful work in the Kingdom of God may not be the big things you do, but the little people you love." This quote is framed with a picture of our children hanging in the office at Kingdom Kids Home. I want our staff to always know the little things they do each day are making a big difference in the lives of our kids and in the kingdom of God. Each time they serve a child a meal, get them dressed, or say a pray before bedtime, they are training the next generation of leaders and producing young world changers. That is no small task!

A few days later, our missions team finally arrived. Since I had dreamed of taking missionaries on trips with my own organization since I was fourteen years old, I was still in awe it was actually happening!

The night before the home opened, we had a night of prayer where our team dedicated the house to Lord. I remember sitting alone in the corner of the courtyard praying. I got down on my knees and my prayer went something like this: "Lord, this home is a testimony and evidence of your faithfulness. It is living proof of how you can use a normal 18-year-old girl with a God-given dream to do something beautiful for Your kingdom. Thank You Lord. This home is Yours, and all of this is for Your glory." I prayed the prayer I wrote about in my prayer journal that I promised God I would pray when the home opened. This was such a surreal moment for me. I could not believe I was here. Tomorrow,

I would reach my destination. Kingdom Kids Home would open its doors for the first time and welcome 16 children into their brand new home. This could not be real.

The next morning came, and the big day was here! June 28, 2015 had finally arrived, and I had countless thoughts running through my head. It was our first, full day together as a missions team. In a few hours, I was going to meet the very kids I had been dreaming about and praying about for years. Would they show up? Would they run into the house like I envisioned? Would they even like us? Those were just a couple of the thoughts circulating through my brain. I'd be lying if I said I was not a little bit nervous. But, before I knew it, our team was loading up the bus and heading over to the orphanage for the grand opening.

We pulled up to the house, exited the bus, and as I walked through our front gate, I saw a bunch of children and families dispersed throughout our yard. They were here! When I saw them, all my nerves and fears immediately left and were replaced with excitement and overwhelming joy! I went around meeting the kids and their family members, relatives, or friends who had brought them to the orphanage. The children looked very surprised when I came up to them and greeted all of them by their first name. Most of the kids were quiet, shy, and not overly affectionate. I noticed one little boy standing all alone, looking at the ground in the corner of our yard. I recognized him from his picture. It was Dorval, our six-year-old boy whose father had murdered his mother and then abandoned him. I was going to make it my mission to love on this boy who had been through so much at just six years old. I walked over to Dorval and introduced myself. I asked him if he wanted to be my buddy, and he slightly nodded. This young boy was so sad and depressed. He never even looked me in the eye. Dorval just stared at the ground the entire time I talked to him, with the saddest expression on his face. He seemed so lifeless. This broke my heart. I decided throughout the course of the week, I was going to make it my mission to restore joy in Dorval's heart.

After all the introductions had been made, it was time to cut the ribbon and officially open the home. The team and the kids crowded around the entry way to the house where my sister had tied a light purple ribbon across the entry way… the same light purple ribbon I had seen in my vision about three and a half years earlier. This was it. I was at my destination. The dream God gave to me on January 3rd, 2012 when I was an 18-year-old college freshman was about to become reality.

Robinson prayed over the house and over the kids. Then, I told the kids I was going to cut the ribbon, and when I cut the ribbon, they were to run into and explore their brand new home! The kids were so excited… a couple of them tried to run in before the ribbon was cut! I joyfully shouted, "Are you guys ready to see your new home?" The kids screamed "Oui!" with so much excitement. They were beyond ready, and believe me, I was too! I turned around, and as I cut the ribbon, I loudly proclaimed, "Welcome to Kingdom Kids Home!"

These beautiful children charged through the freshly cut ribbon and ran into their new home, just like God had showed me they would years before.

It would be impossible to describe the emotions I was feeling in that moment. All I know is it was hands down one of the greatest moments of my life. I was overwhelmed with joy and overwhelmed with gratitude. I could not believe God had brought me here, but I was so thankful He had.

Moments after the ribbon was cut, I too ran into the house with excitement. I wanted to see the kids' reactions as they explored their brand new house. The children were running everywhere, screaming with excitement. I went into the boys bunk room just in time to see Jacky, one of our six year olds, face planting on his brand new bed! As I mentioned earlier, Jacky was our boy who was homeless sleeping on the streets with his father every night. This was his first bed and I was so glad I got to witness his reaction first hand! Then I looked across the room and Holando, our 10 year old, and the oldest in the house, climbed up to the top bunk, sat down, smiled, and gave me a big thumbs up. I loved seeing the kids jump on their brand new beds… just like God showed me they would in the vision He put on my heart years before.

After the kids explored the house for a while, it was time to give them gifts! We bought each child a brand new backpack and our teamed stuffed each backpack with toys and school supplies. Watching the kids receive their brand new backpacks was my favorite moment of the day. The kids seemed surprised they were getting yet another gift. I stood against the wall in the living room and watched as the children ripped open their new backpacks and began to shriek with excitement and joy as they saw all the toys inside of them. As I quietly stood back, observing the beautiful scene, I thought to myself, Wow, it does not get any better than this. I reflected on the journey, on getting to this point. I remembered having the initial dream and thinking, No way. I remembered God speaking to me on the flight home from my 2012 Haiti trip where he told me Haiti was definitely the spot we would put the home. I remembered slowly sharing my story with key people, praying they would not think I was insane. I remembered getting shot down and laughed at by Joe. I remembered the time I contacted random builders who I did not even know. I remembered meeting Robinson down a dirt road, backstreet in Haiti where I nervously asked him if he would like to be involved in the orphanage. I remembered pulling up to the house for the first time, knowing it was the spot. Tears ran my down my face, and I quietly said to myself, "Wow, this moment right here made it so worth it." All of the heart ache, happiness, craziness, confusion, pain, moments of victory and moments of defeat I had experienced along the road—I would do it all over again just to be here in that moment.

Soon after the gifts were opened, our team gathered the kids outside on the back patio area, which was now the devotional and Bible lesson area. The most important moment of the day had arrived—it was time to introduce our kids to Jesus! I shared the simple gospel message with our 16 children, and at the end, I presented the opportunity for the kids to accept Christ into their hearts. On the first day of Kingdom Kids Home, every one of our children raised their hand to accept Christ and to make Jesus the Lord of their life. Right after each child prayed the prayer of salvation, our team gave them brand new Bibles.

That opening day is one I will never forget. Through the week that followed, the children who used to be names and faces pasted on a document quickly became family to me. Day by day, the kids began to open up. As the week went by, there was a lot more laughter, dancing, and hugs. The kids became very attached to the team, literally. They would not let us put them down once we were holding them. Each child's unique personality slowly began to peek through what was once a tough and unapproachable exterior. In just one week, the kids were learning what it looked like to love and be loved. They now had a family. A place where they were safe, loved, and cared for. A place where they did not have to worry about where their next meal would come from or even if they would have a next meal. A place where they knew exactly where they were going to rest their heads at night. A place where they were considered sons and daughters—not only of Robinson and the Kingdom Kids Home staff, but sons and daughters of the most high God.

My favorite transformation to witness was sweet Dorval. As I mentioned before, he had been very quiet, isolated, and depressed. He would not talk to anyone, and he spent most of the day staring at the ground. A few hours into opening day, Dorval's demeanor had already begun to change. When each child was opening his brand new backpack, Dorval came alive! He was so thrilled about his new house and new gift that he began speaking rather profusely in Creole. My sister, Shelby, noticed this and asked a translator what Dorval was saying. The translator asked Dorval, "What do you need, buddy?" Dorval replied, "What do I need? I have house, a backpack, a bed, new toys, and new friends… I don't need anything else!" From that point on, life was restored into Dorval's young soul. The rest of the week he was laughing, being goofy, and talking out of turn most of the time… but we did not mind. We were just happy to see Dorval come alive!

Our first trip was an incredible one. Our team discipled and taught the Kingdom Kids different Bible lessons everyday, visited children's ministries around Haiti, and put on nights of ministry at different churches around Port Au Prince. Before I knew it, the week had flown by and our team was headed back to America. I was thankful to be heading home after a very busy trip, filled with many emotions, but it was definitely tough to leave my kids.

I came to Haiti prepared to meet 16 new children and left with 16 new family members.

Now, as you can imagine, my relationship with each child has only grown stronger. I Skype in for each of their birthday parties and have actually been down in Haiti to attend a couple of them. I know Holando loves Captain America and Oliviero loves Batman. I know Jacky is dying for me to get him a remote control motorcycle for his birthday… we'll see if that happens! I know Nataelle, our youngest boy, will beg you to hold him every time he sees you, and once you've got him, he will not let you put him down. I know Shaniaka is obsessed with dolls with pretty hair and our little Judeline dances like she just got off the set of a Beyonce video! That girl is always the life of the party! I know Jeffly loves sports and is a rising basketball star. I know every child loves going to school and they proudly show off their school uniforms. I also know all the kids love going to the beach and keep asking Robinson when they're going to go back!

Honestly, these children are the greatest thing that has ever happened to me. I now know a depth of love I did not even know existed. I feel like the richest person alive. There is a lot of joy in running Kingdom Kids Home. But, what I do not share quite as often with people is along with the joys, there is also a fair share of struggles. Running a ministry is not always easy. In fact, in the past year and a half that Kingdom Kids Home has been open, I am pretty sure I have hit my knees more than ever before. There have been times where I have needed thousands of dollars by the end of the month and no clue how we were going to come up with it. But, through it all, I have learned the truth of Psalm 46:1-7 still reigns true.

> God is our refuge and strength, an ever-present help in trouble. Therefore we will not fear, though the earth give way and the mountains fall into the heart of the sea, though its waters roar and foam and the mountains quake with their surging. There is a river whose streams make glad the city of God, the holy place where the Most High dwells. God is within her, she will not fall; God will help her at break of day. Nations are in uproar, kingdoms fall; he lifts his voice, the earth melts. The Lord Almighty is with us; the God of Jacob is our fortress.

Through it all, God has been with me. He has always and will always take care of me. Because when you say "yes" to God and take bold steps forward, following after your dream, He will not leave you hanging. As I have said before and still believe today, living a life of obeying God and saying yes to the crazy things He is calling you to do is the best way to live. When you do such things, you will live a very, very rich life—not one reflected by the amount that sits in your bank account. But, one reflected by the amount of love and joy in your heart.

Mother Teresa said it best, "I think a person who is attached to riches, who lives with the worry of riches, is actually very poor. However, if a person puts their money at the service of others, then they are rich, very rich."

Personal Journal Entry:

June 28, 2015

Wow... words cannot really express the overwhelming joy I felt when meeting the kids today! It was so cool to see their faces and to meet the little ones I have been praying about for quite some time now! They were all so sweet! One of my favorite moments of the day was to see the vision God gave me three years ago come to life! When we cut the ribbon, the kids raced into the house, and it was so cool to see them so happy and excited. I'll never forget when our Holando climbed up to the top of his bed, smiled, and gave a big thumbs up! Then, Jacky came in and face planted on his bed with a huge smile! It was awesome to see those kids so happy and for all the hard work and planning to pay off! Then we sat all the kids down and passed out their brand new backpacks filled with goodies! This was my absolute favorite moment! Seeing the huge smiles spread across each face as they ripped open their backpacks was the absolute best! I can't even describe how happy I was in that moment! It truly is more blessed to give than to receive!

  Later, we took all of the children out to the lesson area and told them about Jesus. They all accepted him into their hearts. Then, Robinson read them a story about creation from their brand new Bibles. They loved their Bibles and loved the story. I cannot put into words how incredible today was! God truly is the fulfiller of dreams. We just have to say yes to Him.

The grand opening of Kingdom Kids Home on June 28, 2015!

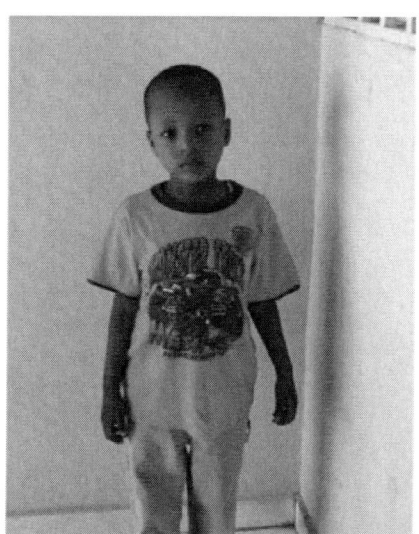

Dorval on the day he came into Kingdom Kids Home.

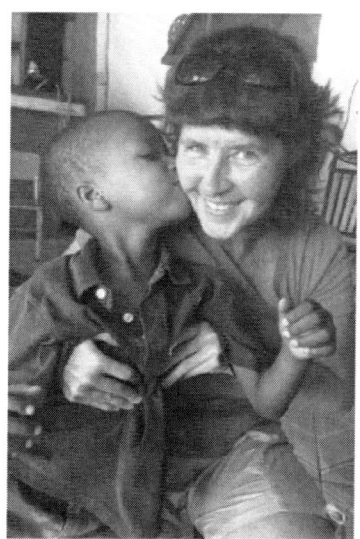 

Dorval's transformation a few days into his life at Kingdom Kids Home!

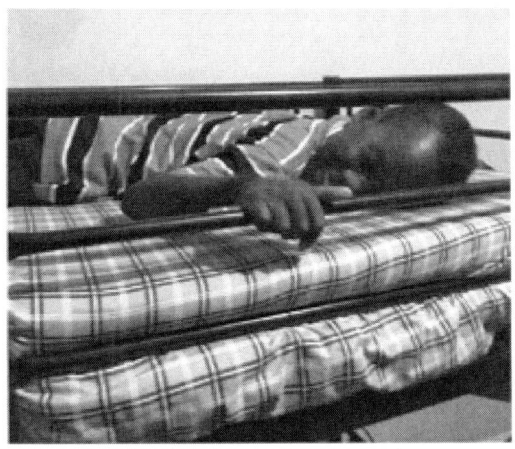

Jacky face planting onto his
brand new bed!

Alexandro and Angelica excited
to receive their new backpacks!

The Kingdom Kids on their first day of school.

Our children praying during their devotional time.

Meet my family!

Chapter 19:
Under the Influence

Whether you realize it or not, you are always influencing someone. And you are influencing them in one of two directions—good or bad, positive or negative, up or down. We have the power to influence every one we interact with.

For example, if you're at the grocery store about to step into the self check out line and the employee overseeing the self checkout says to you, "Um, excuse me, ma'am! Do you see how many items are in your cart?" You look down and notice you have around 16 items. Then, he abruptly points to the sign that reads "no more than 10 items in the self checkout line" and says in an annoyed tone, "There's definitely more then 10 items there. Move to another line!" You think "Well, excuse me sir. I did not notice the sign, my bad." I may or may not be writing this story form a recent experience. But that employee could have nicely asked you to move to another line, and you would have left with a good impression. But he did not, and you left feeling like "Wow, that guy clearly did not have his coffee this morning!"

No matter who you are—the CEO of a company or the guy working a grocery store self-checkout area—you have the power and capability to influence and impact someone's life. The big question is: What kind of influence are you going to make? Will it a good one or a bad one? Positive or negative? Will you push them up and higher towards great things, or will you bring them down?

You can probably tell by now since I have quoted her a few times throughout my book, Mother Teresa is someone I greatly admire. Growing up, I joked I want to be the modern day version of Mother Teresa (and the married version)! What I would give to sit and have a conversation with her. She was a very wise woman who had a huge heart for Jesus, a huge heart for people, and she was a woman who left a huge impact on many people's lives. Her positive influence still lives on today. One thing she said that I often remember and have written down in several journals is: "One day you will just be a memory for someone. Do your best to be a good one." She realized her time with each individual and her time on earth was short—and she was determined to make the most of it.

Mother Teresa started to feel the call of God on her life when she was 18 years old. She decided to become a nun and live a life dedicated to helping other people. Years later, when she was 36 years old, she heard what she refers to as "the call within the call." Mother Teresa was traveling on a train when the Lord gave her new direction telling her she needed to dedicate her life to helping the poorest of the poor in Calcutta, India. She left her teaching job and place of comfort and launched the Missionaries of Charity—an organization dedicated to loving and caring for people living in poverty.

Slowly, Mother Teresa and her sisters in the Missionaries of Charity began to help and take care of people, one person at a time. Over time, Mother Teresa's ministry work began to expand, and God opened door after door for the Missionaries of Charity to impact more lives. The Missionaries of Charity provided food for the poor, gave medical care to people living in the slums, visited the elderly, comforted the dying, gave comfort to the abandoned, and taught children educational lessons and proper hygiene. Even though Mother Teresa has passed, her influence still lives on today through the Missionaries of Charity. Today, the number of Missionaries of Charity's brothers and sisters has grown to more than 4,000 worldwide and is in 123 countries. During her lifetime, Mother Teresa received more than 700 awards, one of the awards being the Nobel Peace Prize.

Cleary, Mother Teresa was a woman of great influence, who impacted thousands of lives during her 87 years on this earth. She knew her time was limited and was determined not to waste her life. Every time I read about Mother Teresa's accomplishments, I am so inspired, and I always pray God might use my young life to impact people the way she did.

I have learned influence is usually a cycle. Usually there is someone who has previously influenced the influencer. There's someone who's told the person impacting lives not to waste their life and who's shown them how to live a life filled with purpose. That was the case with Mother Teresa. Her mother,

Dranafile, modeled to Agnes (who later became Mother Teresa) what it looked like to care for the needs of others. Agnes did not come from a well off family, but she remembered seeing her mother continuously looking after the needs of the sick and the poor. At a young age, Agnes watched her mother bring food to the home of a poor woman every week, and then her mother would clean this woman's house. Her mother took care of another woman whose body was covered in sores. When a poor widow died, Agnes's mom took the woman's children into her own family. She taught Agnes and her siblings the importance of going to church and how to pray. She was a model and positive influence for young Agnes, who would one day become the world renown Mother Teresa.

I did not know Mother Teresa personally, but I bet the reason she grew up having a deep concern and compassion for hurting and broken people was because her mother taught her how to be that way. Thank God Mother Teresa's mother influenced her in the manner she did because if she hadn't, there would be a lot more orphans, homeless, and lost people in the world. I doubt Dranafile even noticed young Agnes was paying such close attention the way she lived her life. But, she impacted Agnes's life in a positive way, then Agnes went on to impact many other lives in a positive way, and hopefully they went on to impact others as well.

Throughout the journey of starting Kingdom Kids Home, many people have influenced my life. From the missionary who spoke in my elementary chapel when I was in first grade, to Hannah who told me a message straight from God on my first visit to Haiti, to pastors and leaders of my missions trips, to professors and leaders at ORU—God knew I would need all these positive influences to catapult me into my future. Many people encouraged me, spoke life in to my dream, and helped move me forward along the path to reaching my destination. But, like Mother Teresa, the two biggest influences in my life have been my parents, Tim and Tammie Chute. These two are the reason I know God. They literally lived out the verse, "Train up a child in the way they should go." (Proverbs 22:6) They are the ones who led me to the Lord in our living room when I was five years old, and they have been leading me closer to Him every day since. They did not just tell me what it was like to be a Christian; they showed me by the way they lived their lives. They sacrificed financially to put me in a Christian school where God first told me to be a missionary. They did not just tell my sisters and me that we needed to go to church. Instead, they were in church every time the doors were open, serving in some capacity. My mom taught my Sunday school classes and my dad served as an elder. They did not just casually talk with people; they genuinely loved people! I remember being the last ones out of church every single Sunday because my parents were still talking. Now, I am the last one out of my church just about every single Sunday for the same reason. The apple does not fall far from the tree. My parents were not one way in private and another way in public. They practiced what they preached. They modeled for my sisters and me what it looked like to be genuine and authentic. They truly loved and respected each other and their children. They have always been supportive of my dreams, no matter how crazy they seemed.

I remember the first time I told my parents about my dream to open an orphanage. They looked surprised at first, but at the end of the conversation my mom just looked at my dad and said, "Well Tim, looks like we better start saving our money because we're going to be headed to Haiti in a few years!" Having their support made me believe in myself. Without the two of them, Kingdom Kids Homes would not exist and there would still be 16 children out on the streets.

If you're a parent, or if you plan on being a parent someday, I want to speak directly to you for a moment. Do not downplay the opportunity you have to influence your child's life. You have been given such a gift. You have the opportunity to raise a world changer. You have the power to show your child what it looks like to live a life pointed to the cross and to live a life fully devoted to Christ. You have the power to build them up and encourage their dreams, and you also have the power to tear them down. Please use that power for good.

Take it from someone who has been there. When you're a parent who does it right, you will raise up a child who dreams God-sized dreams and a child who wants to put their mark on this world for Jesus Christ. Your child will feel like their potential is limitless. And if you need some tips, I can give you my parents number because they did it right.

My prayer is for God to use me to influence others in the right way. I want to be someone who points people towards Jesus in every area of my life. When people leave me, I want them to feel lifted up and full of joy. I want to believe in people's dreams, and push them forward on the path to following them, just like so many people did for me.

My big vision with Kingdom Kids Homes is to raise up children all over Haiti, and maybe someday around the world, to know their place in the kingdom of God and then to teach those children to go out and bring others into the kingdom.

At Kingdom Kids Home, we are already beginning to do just that. With every trip to Haiti, I love seeing how much our children have grown, not only physically, but in their relationship with the Lord. Our home has only been open for a year and a half and our kids are already so in love with Jesus. Now, when we take mission trips down to Haiti, the kids come with us on every outreach, and they become a part of the missions team for the week.

Last December, we were hosting a food outreach where we handed out bags of food to families in need of meals at Christmastime. Members from our missions team shared testimonies, and before passing out the food, we went out in groups and prayed for people. The kids joined the various prayer groups and laid hands on people and prayed for their needs. I would take turn calling on the kids in my group, and I would have them voice a prayer out loud for the person we were praying for. The kids would get so excited when I asked them to lead our group in prayer.

During the prayer time, I took a moment to stand back and watch the scene. Tears welled up in my eyes, and I stood back seeing our kids spread all across the ministry area praying for people. I thought to myself, "This is why Kingdom Kids Homes exits." Kingdom Kids was created to teach children how to impact lives for Jesus Christ. And there the Kingdom Kids children were at ages six, seven, and eight already influencing people in a positive way. It was such a beautiful picture of the gospel. God does not care how experienced you are, how long you have been saved, or how old you are. He does not have a list of requirements you have to meet before you can go out and reach people for His kingdom. He only requires childlike faith, and our kids are filled with a lot of it.

When we got back on the bus after the outreach, I asked all of the kids what their favorite part of the outreach was. All of kids responded with the same answer: praying for other people.

It only takes one person to influence someone's life. You might be sitting here reading this thinking, "Well what can I do? I am just a normal person." Well hey, so am I!

Sometimes it can be overwhelming when we look at the whole picture of life. So let me just encourage you to focus on today, this week, or even this season of life you're in. What can you do now to influence someone's life in the right way. You do not have to know the next ten years. Just think about what you can do here and now to influence someone's life. How can you encourage them in their walk with the Lord? How can you inspire and bring about positive change in someone's life? Well all have the power to influence others. You just have to be intentional about doing it and doing it the right way.

As I mentioned before, influence is usually a cycle. I love the story of our orphanage director, Robinson. For a long time he has felt called to run an orphanage for children who would not have a chance at making it on their own. The reason this is Robinson's dream is because of the way one woman impacted his life when he was a young boy. Robinson did not grow up in a wealthy family in Haiti, and his family could not afford to send him to school. One woman saw potential in Robinson. God put it on her heart to help Robinson and to give him the chance to make something out of his life. This woman sponsored all the years of Robinson's education. Due to her generosity, Robinson was given the opportunity to have a very bright future. He also learned to speak English well, due to his education. Since this sweet woman did this for Robinson, he felt God calling him to have an orphanage where he could do the same thing for not just one child but multiple children.

Now, look at Robinson today. He not only runs Kingdom Kids Home, but he coordinates all of the missions projects and work our ministry does in Haiti. He is not only impacting the lives of our 16 kids, but the lives of many children and people in need all over Haiti. This is all due to the *one* woman who influenced Robinson's life in the right way. Now, because of her impact on his life, he is impacting and changing the lives of many. Like I said, it only takes *one*.

You may hear how you influenced someone's life and see how they are going on to impact the lives of others, or you may never know. But picture this: How amazing will it be when our lives on earth end and we walk through heaven's gate. God will welcome you in and say, "Hey, I have to show you something." He takes you into a library and pulls a catalog out of a shelf. You'll examine the book and boy, it's thick! You'll then realize it has your name on it and the subtitles will read "Catalog of Influence." God will open it up and you'll go through it with Him, page by page, and see all the people you have influenced for the kingdom during your time on earth. You'll flip through each page with amazement because half of the people in there you did not even know about! What a glorious moment that will be.

But first, you have to make the choice. You have to choose to be intentional about impacting and influencing lives for Jesus Christ during the limited time you have on earth.

Here's one final quote from Mother Teresa. This happens to be my all time favorite quote and it impacts my heart every time I read it:

"Spread love every where you go. Let no one come ever come to you without leaving better or happier. Be the living expression of God's kindness."

Now, let me close this chapter with wisdom straight from the man who was biggest influencer of all time. Jesus said, "In the same way, let your light shine before others, that they may see your good deeds and glorify your Father in heaven." (Mathew 5:16)

As believers, it is our mission to spread the love of Christ. It is our mission to show God's kindness. It is our mission to let our light shine in a dark world.

We all have the power to influence. How will you use yours?

Personal Journal Entry from My Prayer Journal:

September 24, 2015

My Sweet Jesus,

Thank you for who You are and what You did for this world, but more importantly, thank You for who You are to me. When I think about You, Jesus, there is nothing that even comes close in comparison. You, God, are so beautiful in all Your ways. Let me be a reflection of that beauty to everyone around me. You have such a heart, love, and compassion for people… especially people who do not even care to know You. You still fight for them, and You still love them. Give me that kind of love, a love that has such compassion for people, even people all over this world I might not even know.

    I thank You that while You were here on earth, You modeled what it looked like to be a servant. I pray You can grow in me a heart to serve others and to go the extra mile for people without expecting anything in return.

    God, I thank You for being my miracle worker and provider. I cannot think of a time where I had a serious need for something and You did not meet it. Especially with Kingdom Kids Home. Who but you could orchestrate such a crazy story of how I got the house and the orphanage director? Who else could line everything up so perfectly and have all the details in place? Only You, my miracle working Jesus. Let me never fail to give You the credit, the praise, and all the glory.

Thank you for being the generator of all my visions and big dreams. While most of the dreams You consistently put on my heart are intimidating, scary, and way beyond myself, I thank You for them, and I would not have it any other way. Ever since I was 13 years old, I have always prayed You would use me to do big things, and that I would not just live an average life. I thank You for answering that prayer, but I also thank You that You're not done yet, but that this is only just the beginning of the work You're doing in me and through my life.

My life is wholly yours. Use it for your glory always.

Amen.

Chapter 20:
In His Strength

If you asked me today if launching Kingdom Kids Homes and opening our first home was the best thing I have ever done, I would say, "Yes." Knowing you are following after and walking out exactly what God has called you to do is truly the greatest feeling in the world.

My life has changed in little and big ways since the opening of Kingdom Kids Home. Now when I scan the shoe section at Target, I often find myself looking at the kids section first to see if there's any cute little sandals on clearance before I ever make it over to my own section! If I have some extra money, I now find myself heading to the toy section to buy a remote control helicopter to surprise the kids with on my next visit to Haiti. Most people think, "Wow you did it! You opened an orphanage. That's awesome! You raised all that money, and you completed the task. Way to go!" And that's the end of the story. In reality, nothing could be further from the truth. In the weeks and months following the opening of our home, I started to feel like the real work was actually just beginning.

Starting an orphanage is not just something you can do and then just check out. After it opens, the pressure is really on because now you have 16 mouths to feed and enroll and put through school and to take to the doctor for routine check ups and buy clothes, shoes, and other basic needs for. Oh, and you also have a staff of 10 plus employees under you who expect to receive a salary every single month. Oh, and you have to pay bills on the house so simple things like the water and electricity stay on. Yeah, now you can see how I was feeling the pressure.

So, while opening and running a children's home is extremely exciting and fulfilling, it's also extremely scary at times. In fact, I know for certain I have not hit my knees, relying on God to come through for me, more than I have since we opened the home.

I have never felt so nervous and scared about something as the time I did when we went to enroll our kids in school the first year. Maybe I am naive or maybe I was just inexperienced (Okay, I was definitely inexperienced.), but I received the school prices and realized they were about 5,000 more dollars than we had budgeted for. About three weeks before I had to send the funds down to enroll our children in school for the first year, Robinson informed me the Christian school we were looking to put our children in had raised their school prices and we needed to come up with an extra 5,000 dollars to send our kids to school there! I had a minor panic attack.

Five thousand dollars? I did not have that kind of money lying around. And I had no idea how I was supposed to raise that in three weeks. After I got off of my Skype call with Robinson, I began to feel sick to my stomach and all at once this huge wave of stress came over my body. I thought, Oh my gosh, you open this children's home, promising to give children a Christian education, and it's only been open for two and half months and you can't even put them in school!

For the next few weeks I was overwhelmed, and I had this deep weight hanging on me. I tried to do normal things, like hang out with my friends, but every time I did something fun, that huge cloud of uncertainty and pressure as to how I was going to raise that kind of money that little amount of time hovered over me. I prayed a ton and begged God to provide some miracle for us. One thing I did know for certain: I was not going to give up. Once again, I had to choose to let my faith outweigh my fears. I had to choose to have faith God would provide.

I messaged so many of my friends asking if each of them would just make a one time donation of 25 dollars to help send the kids to school. So many people responded and many people donated more than 25 dollars. Then, Robinson called me and told me he found another Christian school in the same neighborhood as our house, that he actually liked better than the original school we were looking at. And best of all, it was about 2,000 dollars cheaper than the first school! Praise the Lord!

I trusted Robinson's judgment, and I also liked the pricing of the second Christian school way better than the first, so

I said we would go with that one! That news took a weight off my shoulders, and after hearing it, I knew God's favor was shining upon us! Also, during the three weeks we had to come up with the money for school, we had two pretty random, large, one-time donations come in. Between the large handful of my friends who gave a one time donations of 25 dollars or more, the second school having lower prices, and the two unexpected large one time donations, we had raised the extra money we needed for school within the three weeks we needed it. I sent the funds down, and we were able to send our children to school for the first time in their lives.

Those few weeks were crazy and such a whirlwind. Honestly, I never want to feel that panicked and overwhelmed again. But, like always, my God came through. As if I haven't said this enough throughout this book: That is just what our God does. When we put ourselves out there, when we say "yes" to what God is asking us to do, and when we take steps of faith toward following Him, He will not leave us hung out to dry. He will always take care of us.

And while managing a ministry isn't always easy, I can confidently tell you there has never been a time when God has not come through for us. When it comes time to send the support funds down each month, we have never come up short. Sometimes that in itself is a miracle, and I have to stop and think, "Um, where is this money coming from?" But, it always shows up. Better yet, God always shows up. Every single time!

About a month after the scare of the school prices, I was driving in my car alone, having a silent convo with God. I was silently saying, "God, I love running Kingdom Kids Homes, and it is the biggest blessing to me, but is it always going to be this hard? It feels like a constant roller coaster. One moment things are going great, and the next, I am wondering how we're going to make it through the month. I honestly thought it would be easier than this." Then, I heard God speak to my heart as clear as day. He said, "Kristie, I know it's hard. But it needs to be hard so you keep depending on me. The moment things get easy and you think you can coast, that's when you start to take your eyes off me. You start to put your confidence in yourself and not in me. I am making it hard and difficult here in the beginning so you learn to constantly depend on me, and so you realize you cannot do this alone. I will come through for you every time. But it needs to be hard so you learn I am your source of strength and you cannot do this without me."

I thought, Wow, well… that answered that question! I knew He was right. The minute things were looking good, I prayed less. I consulted with myself before making decisions and not God. I would start to go with the plans I had in mind instead of following after His direction and leading.

I learned the hard way (and am still learning), God is my source of strength. Without Him I am nothing, have nothing, and can do nothing. When God is calling you to do something with your life, whether it be big or small, you need to seek the Lord for strength, help, and guidance every step of the way. He is the true source.

Even Jesus knew this. Jesus, the son of God, recognized his need for God's strength when he was preparing to go to the cross to take on the sins of the world. Moments before Jesus was arrested and taken to be crucified, he prayed in the Garden of Gethsemane. In the book of Luke it says:

> Jesus withdrew about a stones throw beyond them, knelt down, and prayed. 'Father if you are willing, take this cup from me; yet not my will, but yours be done.' An angel of heaven appeared and strengthened him. And being in anguish, he prayed more earnestly, and his sweat was like drops of blood falling to the ground.
>
> Luke 22:41-44 (NIV)

Being crucified for the sins of the world is no small task. Jesus clearly was not excited about being put to death in the most excruciating way possible, but He knew it was what God called Him to do. So He went to the source. He asked God to give Him the strength to complete his own scary and overwhelming call. He recognized He could not do it alone. I love how it says an angel from heaven strengthened Him. This shows us when we call on God for strength, recognize our need for Him, and ask Him for help, He will meet us where we're at, and He will strengthen us.

No one is above asking God for strength. Even Jesus, the holy, perfect, Son of God, knew He could not complete God's purpose for His earthly life without the Father's help.

The Bible says, "Seek first his kingdom and his righteousness, and all these things will be given to you as well." (Matthew 6:33, NIV) God wants to see you succeed, and when you are intentional about putting His ways and His desires above your own, He will give you more than you could have ever dreamed about.

Now, every time I take trips down to Haiti, so many people ask me to help them. Different pastors, mothers, fathers, leaders in the community, you name it. I get asked to adopt all different kinds of projects. Haiti is a nation with a lot of need, and people there are so desperate for someone to help them.

On my last trip, one of the leaders in a community we frequently minister to on trips asked to have a special meeting with me. I assumed he was sitting down with me to ask me to adopt one of his projects…and I was right. He presented me with his plan, and at the end of his talk, he wanted me to give him a yes or no answer on the spot. I said to him, "Thank you for sharing all this with me. I will be praying about it." I don't think my vague answer was the one he was looking for. He said, "Miss Kristie, please let me know if you will help." I said, "There is no way I can let you know if I can help today. I do not make those decisions." He looked at me with a funny look. I read his expression, and I think it said, "But, you're in charge here aren't you?" I went on to explain to him that I am not the one who decides what projects we adopt or what the next moves for Kingdom Kids Homes will be. That is God's job, and I simply just listen to him. He is the one who puts ideas, plans, and visions on my heart. I told this sweet man every project we chose to adopt or every new person or place we decided to help was because God told me to. I said to this leader, "I only do a project if God tells me to. If I just do what I want to do then I am following after my own plan and God is not in it. But, if I am following after God's plan, He will make a way. He will open the doors we need, and He will make it successful because it is His vision. I am simply choosing to obey and follow after it. If I make the decision to do something without letting Christ lead me, it will fail because I am operating out of my own strength and not His."

And that has been one of the most important lessons I have learned when it comes to running Kingdom Kids Homes and when it comes to running my own life. They are both God's, so why don't I let Him be in the drivers seat?

Every decision we make in life, ministry, relationships, jobs, etc. should be directed and pioneered by Him. After all He is the one who created us, so I think He'll know what's best for us. And with Kingdom Kids, He's the one who told me to start it, so I think He'll know what is best for that too.

When we operate with Christ as our source of strength, the pressure is taken off. We do not need to worry about how things will come together or how things will work out. We just need to worry about following Him, and believe me, He will do a great job at figuring out the rest.

Personal Journal Entry from My Missions Journal:

December 14, 2015

Well, we're back at it, again! I am on a flight now heading to Haiti with a team of missionaries who are pumped to bring the joy of Jesus and Christmas to so many Haitians this week! I still cannot believe I get to lead missions teams with my very own ministry! How did I get here? It feels like I was just 14 yesterday, fighting for my passport to come in so I could make it on my first trip to Guatemala. I love looking back and seeing how God has constantly had His hand on so many different areas of my life. His goodness will never cease to amaze me!

Well, this trip we'll be giving a lot of ourselves, and I am so excited about that!

This is my focus for this week, and I get so excited knowing this is what God says about me:

"I took you, Kristie, from the ends of the earth. From the farthest corners, I have called you! I have said, you, Kristie, are my servant. I have chosen you and have not rejected you. So do not fear, Kristie, for I am with you. Do not be dismayed, for I am your God. I will strengthen you and I will help you; I will uphold you with my right hand" (Isaiah 41:9-10 The Kristie Version).

I am so thankful to serve a God who is constantly calling me to greater things, who upholds me, and strengthens me when I am weak. And I am thankful my God is always with me...no matter where I go. He is ever faithful. I am so excited and expectant to see the ways He uses our team in Haiti this week! May it blow my mind!

Chapter 21:
Keep Dreamin'

I have always considered myself to be a dreamer, and I am happy to inform you, I still am!

I will forever be amazed at the journey God had me on in order to reach my destination. I have grown in big ways and have learned many new things. I took bold steps of faith, put myself out there, trusted God; and He proved Himself faithful. It has been an incredible ride. And I am so glad this is only just the beginning!

I know there is so much more God wants to do through me personally and through Kingdom Kids Homes. Before we even opened the first Kingdom Kids Home, God was already starting to put new dreams and new visions on my heart for the future. I remember thinking, Slow down God! I just want to open this first house and get it successfully up and running! I am not ready to hear about the next thing! Hearing next steps when you are just trying to complete the first one can be pretty overwhelming. I remember thinking, Can I just get like a week off? Or a short break?

Then I realized, just like influence, dreams are also a cycle. First, you will be in the "what's next" phase. This is the phase where you asking what God's dream for your life is and where you are seeking and asking him what you are supposed to do next. Then, God will place a dream on your heart, and you are in the "follow me" stage. In this stage, you have to choose to embrace the dream and the burden God is putting on your heart, and you have to choose to obey Him and start to go after it. Then, once you are in the midst of your journey and on the road to having your God-given dream become reality, you are in the "trust me" phase. You have to choose to trust God will make a way for you, open the right doors, and plop the things you need right in your lap. Even when things are not looking good, you have to choose to trust. Then, the final phase is the "praise me" phase. This is the phase where you get to celebrate! It's where you reach your destination, and you get to give God all the glory and praise. And, if you're a dreamer, like me, after all those phases are complete, you'll head back into the "what's next" phase where you begin to ask God to put another kingdom-sized dream on your heart.

That's where I am at now. This past year I have been in the "what's next" phase. I realized there will never be a season in my life where I am not asking for or going after a God-given dream. And quite honestly, I don't want there to be. I know I am young, 23 to be exact, but I do not know when my time on earth is going to be up. It could be 60 days from now or it could be 60 years from now. What I do know is I want to use whatever time I've got here on earth to do big things for the Kingdom of God. To do things that blow my mind and greatest expectations. I still pray the same prayer as when I was thirteen and fourteen, and I plan on praying it for the rest of my life. "God I do not want to be normal! Use to me to do crazy things for your kingdom."

At Kingdom Kids Home, we are already teaching our children to pray those kinds of prayers and to dream big dreams. You may remember, back in chapter 5, I mentioned that God told me to have a "Dream Day" with the children at Kingdom Kids Home. I am thrilled to let you know we had "Dream Day" on our first trip missions trip back when we opened our house, and we have one "Dream Day" on every missions trip we take down to Haiti!

On our grand opening missions trip, the final thing our missions team did before saying goodbye to the kids was "Dream Day." To be honest with you, I was nervous about doing it. It was something God had laid on my heart to do for some time, and I knew the Lord was directing me to do it. But a lot of the kids were so young, and they had just gotten out of horrible home lives. I did not think they would even respond if I asked them what their dream for their life was. I actually assumed a lot of them would ask, "What does having a dream even mean?" But, I knew God had specifically told me to do it with the Kingdom Kids years before. I also wanted to set the tone for the house right from the beginning. Encouraging our children they were never too young to dream God-sized dreams and to do big things in the Kingdom of God is a huge part of the mission and vision of Kingdom Kids Homes. I wanted to set that tone and atmosphere during the first week our house was alive, so I knew we had to do "Dream Day."

All of the missionaries sat in a large circle with our kids on the back patio of our house. I pointed to the verse I'd had largely painted on the wall of the patio and read it to the kids. It says "Do not let anyone look down on you because you are young, but set an example for the believers in speech, in conduct, in love, in faith, and in purity" (1 Timothy 4:12, NIV). I told our kids they were never to young to follow after God, to hear from God, or to be used by God in a big way. Then, I shared a quick version of my testimony with the kids about how God told me when I was very young, six years old to be exact, the dream and plan He had for my life. I told the kids that God had told me way back then He wanted me to be a missionary, where I helped people and led people to Jesus. And then I told the kids, that was exactly what I was doing here today.

Then, I nervously asked the kids what their dreams were or what they wanted to do with their lives. I nervously waited for 10 seconds, which felt like 10 minutes, for someone to raise his hand and answer. I was thinking, Lord, at least let one kid have a dream here! Then, our sweet Holando, who was ten and the oldest boy in the house, raised his hand. I called on him, and he said he had the dream to be a pastor when he grew up. I was amazed! What an incredible dream. All at once, our whole missions team began to speak life into

Holando's dream. Everyone came around him and told him he was going to be an amazing pastor one day! And let me tell you, he is. I can already see the call of God all over his life! Holando is such a leader and great big brother to all the kids at our house. He already has such a heart of compassion for people and such a love for the Lord. Usually, when we do nights of ministry at churches around Port Au Prince, I have Holando come on stage with me to say the closing prayer for the evening. He always jumps at the opportunity to pray from the stage, and to be quite honest, he always prays a better prayer than I would have prayed! I'm always overflowing with joy when Holando prays in front of a church because I love being able to give him a little taste of what his future holds, while he is only ten years old!

After Holando raised his hand and shared his dream, many other hands started going up. One by one, our children shared their dreams, and after each dream was shared, our missions team would lift up and encourage that dream. Our little Jeffly wants be a woodworker. Jacky wants to be a nurse. Dalinchy, Josue, and Angelica all want to be doctors. Oliviero also wants to be a pastor. Mikenlove wants to be a mechanic, and Alexandro wants to be a police officer. Michelove wants to be a dress-maker. Judeline wants to be president, and Dorval took it one step farther saying he wants to be the President of the United States! I am never one to crush someone's dream, but I'm not sure if that last one is possible. (Although in truth, I would not put it past God!) I reassured him he would be an incredible leader one day!

At the end, our team prayed over the kids' dreams. Now, every time we go back, "Dream Day" is my favorite part of the trip! I love encouraging our kids while they're still young to start dreaming God-sized dreams. I always remind them that they are never too young to start pursuing the call of God on their lives. That is the goal of Kingdom Kids Home. To teach children how to be disciples of Jesus Christ and to raise them up to be the next generation of leaders who can change their nation for the kingdom. Nothing gets me more fired up than seeing this already happening in the lives of our kids when they are only, five, six, and seven years old. I cannot wait to see what they're like when they're 15, 16, and 17 years old!

Dreams are a beautiful thing. I pray you have one already, stirring in your heart. And if you do not, I pray this book inspired you to hop into the "what's next" phase and to begin praying for God to give you a clear vision for your life. One of the things I love the most about dreams is how no two dreams look the same. God has unique visions and plans for everyone and they usually look different from one person to the next. Think about this: could you imagine if everyone in the world pursued and followed after the dream God had placed on their hearts? If you ask most people if they have or once had a dream for their life, people usually have an answer. People usually have something in mind they would do if they knew they could not fail. What would the world be like if everyone chose to fully embrace his or her wildest dream? What would life be like if people chose to not let their fears and uncertainties hold them back from pursing what they felt called to do? How much more beautiful of a place would our world be?

Even though the dream of Kingdom Kids Homes came true, I have still not reached my final destination. I still have more dreams, visions, and ideas God has placed on my heart to do. My final destination will be in heaven, when I hear my heavenly father say: "Good job, Kristie. You obeyed me; you sought me, followed me, even when it was tough. In you I am well pleased. Well done good and faithful servant."

I want to leave you with one final note of encouragement. Do not leave this earth wondering, what would have happened if you had followed your God given dream.

What would have happened if you had embraced the burden God had put on your heart. What would have happened if you had said "yes" to what God was calling you to do?

Say yes. Embrace the dream. Go the distance. Take the journey. Reach your destination. And live your life here on earth with no regrets!

Personal Journal Entry from My Prayer Journal:

August 19, 2015

Dear Heavenly Father,

I pray I never fail to dream big dreams or to pray bold prayers. Even though believing for big things and trusting in You for bold prayers to come to life may be extremely nerve wracking and scary, I thank You it is so worth it. Man, God, there is no better feeling than bringing people closer to Your heart, whether is a child, someone my age, an adult, an elderly person, a homeless person, or the richest man in the world. Give me the tools, open doors, and resources to always bring people closer to Your heart. Use me to help people know You better. Life for me is pretty worthless if I'm not doing that.

God, I thank You for allowing me to see the dream of Kingdom Kids Home come to life. I thank You for constantly making the way for us, and I thank You that You will always continue to do so. Kingdom Kids Homes, our children, our team, and our ministry are Yours! I thank You and trust You will provide for our every last need so we will have the capacity to expand our ministry and to touch and change many more lives for Your glory! I thank You for seeing my dreams and greatest desires. I thank You for placing *them in the depths of my heart for a specific reason. I thank You for making the way and for putting the right people in my path to make them happen. I thank You this is only the beginning!*

God, let me keep You in the forefront of my mind. Let me keep You always at the center and as the number one priority of everything I do. I love You, Lord... so much! You are great. You are good. You are a holy God! But, best of all, You are my God!

Wow, what a privilege that is! All is for Your glory!

Amen.

The Next Step

Our God is a miracle working God, and I hope this story was proof of that! God has big dreams and plans for each of our lives. We simply need to ask Him what that plan is. He desires to know you, have a personal relationship with you, and to use your life to do big things for His Kingdom.

If you do not know the Lord but would like to have a personal relationship with Him, today is the perfect day to start! All it takes is for you to pray a simple prayer, asking Jesus to come into your heart and to be the Lord of your life.

All it takes is praying the following pray and believing it in your heart.

Dear Heavenly Father,
I recognize I do not know you and would like to have a relationship with you. I recognize that I am not perfect and that I have sinned. I believe you forgave those sins when you sent your son, Jesus, to die on a cross for me. Come into my heart today. I believe you are the one true God. Be the Lord of my life. I want to know you, and I

want to follow you for the rest of my life. Thank you for loving me. Now, in turn, I give you my heart, and I want to love you forever.

In Jesus Name,
Amen.

I would love to hear about your personal decisions or the next steps you have taken after reading *The Daring Destination!* Please send me an email at kristie@kristiechute.com so I can celebrate with you!

Your Friend,
Kristie Chute

Acknowledgments

Throughout the journey of launching Kingdom Kids Homes and writing this book, there have been so many people who have come alongside me to help me reach my destination.

Dreamers and visionaries cannot do it alone. It takes a plethora of people who will encourage you, pray for you, travel with you, and help connect you with the right people to get you on the path to reaching your dream. My heart is overwhelmed with joy and gratitude when I think of all of the people who have helped me. There are far too many to name here.

I want to start by thanking my publishers. The Barefoot team is the greatest in the world. I am so glad the story of Kingdom Kids Homes inspired you to step out and say yes to your own God-given dream! You did it! I am proud of you for boldly pursuing and obeying what God has called you to do, and I am grateful for your friendship!

I want to thank everyone at Oral Roberts University who influenced and touched my life during my four years there.

Thank you to all of my professors, deans, hall directors, and faculty members who constantly encouraged me and showed what it looks like to go into every man's world and to make no little plans. I especially want to thank Bob Beard. Thank you for listening to all of my plans and for always being supportive!

Thank you to all the pastors and church congregations who believed in Kingdom Kids Homes when it was only just a dream.

Pastor Tony Rea, thank you taking a young girl with a massive dream into your office one afternoon and for letting me share my God-sized dreams with you! And to everyone at Community Christian Church, thank you for supporting and praying for Kingdom Kids Homes!

Also, to my Gathering, now Anthem Church, family, thank you all for fully supporting me and for praying for me as I was making my way along the path to my destination. I especially want to thank my Pastor, Brad Jenkins. Thank you for seeing a little bit of potential in me and for giving me the opportunity to start working in ministry from a young age. Serving under your leadership over the past few years has been the biggest blessing to me and I have learned so much from you!

I want to thank my Bible study girls—Reiley, Kennedy, Claire, Maggie, Amanda, Caroline, Brooke, and Maloree—and all your families! Thank you for always encouraging me and for supporting my dreams!

To all of my friends who listened to me, encouraged me, and prayed for me along the journey of starting Kingdom Kids, thank you! You know who you are.

Acknowledgments

To my Kingdom Kids Homes family and leadership team: God truly knew I needed each of you in my life, and the ministry would be not be thriving today without all of you!

Thank you to our Haitian staff team who is on the ground every day, working so hard! Thank you for intentionally investing yourselves in our kids lives. You are the real world changers!

Thank you to Kirah and JJ Johnson for being my travel buddies and fellow visionaries when it comes to sharing the story of Kingdom Kids Homes and leading missions teams. I love being a team, and it is the best feeling to know I am not in this alone.

A huge thank you to our orphanage directors, Robinson and Darlene Remedor. Darlene, thank you for continuously loving on our kids and for taking such good care of them. Thank you for being such a strong source of support for Robinson. Robinson, Kingdom Kids Homes would not be in existence if it was not for you! So grateful God gave me you and in the perfect timing. I know this is only just the beginning for us!

Thank you to my amazing siblings! Bryce, I am so glad I finally got a brother after wanting one for years! Thank you for always be so encouraging and supportive of Kingdom Kids Homes! To my younger sister Melissa, thank you for blurting out my dream to start an orphanage to Pastor Tony back in 2013. Thank you for being my biggest cheerleader! To my older sister, Shelby, thank you for believing in my dream and for supporting it from the very start! You believed in me when I did not believe in myself. I am so grateful God gave me a best friend and sister like you!

Thank you to my biggest heroes, supporters, and best friends, my parents, Tim and Tammie Chute. I wouldn't even know Jesus without the two of you. You both are the reason I know God and have the relationship with Him that I do. Thank you for not saying I was crazy when I shared with you my dream to start an orphanage in Haiti. If you wouldn't have believed in me, that probably would have been the end of the road. I love you both so much!

Finally, thank you to the One who gives me the crazy dreams and who fulfills them all, my Lord and Savior Jesus Christ. All of this is because of You and for You. Thank You for leading me, seeing me, and for caring to know me. I love You, and my heart is forever Yours.

About the Author

Kristie Chute is the founder and president of Kingdom Kids Homes, a nonprofit ministry whose mission is to bring children into the kingdom of God and empower and equip them to bring others into the kingdom of God. Kingdom Kids Homes opened their first orphanage in June 2015 to sixteen children in Bon Repos, Haiti.

Kristie grew up in Troy, Michigan and moved to Tulsa, Oklahoma to attend her dream school, Oral Roberts University in the fall of 2011 where she pursued a bachelor's degree in Theology. Currently, she resides in Tulsa and serves on staff at Anthem Church as the director of their next generation ministries and adult connections.

To those who know Kristie best, she's a girl who loves Jesus, making new friends, her family, traveling, sunshine, and coffee! Kristie is passionate about going after the God-sized dreams the Lord places on her heart and believes it is her mission to equip, encourage, and empower others to do the same.

Connect with Kristie!

I pray The Daring Destination inspired and challenged you to dream big dreams. I would love to hear how the book impacted you! I would be honored to answer any questions you may have after reading the book or encourage you in any way I can! Please send me an email at kristie@kristiechute.com and I will personally respond to you!

Follow Kristie:

www.kristiechute.com
www.instagram.com/kristiechute
www.twitter.com/kristiechute
www.pinterest.com/kristiechute

"Let the little children come to me, and do not hinder them, for the kingdom of God belongs to such as these."
Mark 10:14

Kingdom Kids Homes mission is to bring children into the kingdom of God and empower and equip them to bring others into the kingdom of God.

Donate to Kingdom Kids Homes!
kingdomkidshomes.org/donate

Follow the Story:
kingdomkidshomes.org
facebook.com/kingdomkidshomes
instagram.com/kingdomkidshomes